Because I Love You

The Simplicity of God

William David Swindler

Cover art by Michelangelo, "The Creation of Adam"

DEDICATION

This book is dedicated to my wonderful, patient and loving family; My amazing wife Shelley who has been more to me than mere words can describe and the love of my life. And my two beautiful and talented daughters, Alyson and Liliana who perfectly complete our little family and have individually and together made the love of God so very real. Thank you all for choosing to love me back.

It is also dedicated to all of the people who choose to read this little book. It is my heartfelt prayer that it helps you to find for yourself how the simple love of God can change your life, eternally.

CONTENTS

"For God so loved the world that He gave His only begotten Son, that whoever believes in Him should not perish but have everlasting life.

For God did not send His Son into the world to condemn the world, but that the world through Him might be saved."

John 3:16-17

Introduction

There is but one reason for my writing this book; Love. I have been given a gift that I want to share with you; it was given to me freely and it is offered to you likewise. It's about how to have a relationship with the one true God of the Universe. And although I do discuss religions, I am a firm believer that religions are manmade, relationship is God made. Before I begin, please let me beg you to put aside any bias, any preconceived idea about me or this book and read it with an open mind, more importantly an open heart. Let me tell you that my agenda in this book is to offer information for you to judge and determine if you believe what I am telling you. One of the most important aspects of our human existence is the power to make choices. We get to choose what we believe and act upon it accordingly. It was my choice to write this book, it is your choice as to what you do with the information it contains. I am asking that you listen to your heart because that is where some of the best decisions are made.

There is a considerable amount of information that I can share with you regarding what I know about having a personal relationship with God. And this information is for those who desire to establish a relationship but also for those who already have a relationship and wish to grow closer in that relationship. I am not saying this to sound arrogant, it is simply a result of my lifelong relationship with Him and the multitude of experiences that I have encountered. But I don't want to overwhelm you. The realization that I have come to over the writing and organization of this book is that I should try to synopsize or condense the majority and then expound upon it in later chapters. I do this with the idea that many who are reading this may need just that, something simple at first that hopefully will whet the desire to learn more. And please understand that I am never intending to sound condescending or patronizing so please forgive me if in my zeal to share this information I come across in this fashion. I implore you to continue on in this adventure and agree, disagree, argue, debate, and question what I propose. It is your choice.

It is all about the wonderful God given ability to choose. Thank you for allowing me the opportunity to present my conviction from which you may choose to agree or disagree.

I don't believe in coincidences. I have experienced far too many events in my life that simply cannot be explained away as "chance" or "fate". For instance, I don't believe that you are reading this by accident. I believe that God is reaching out to you, as He continually is, to draw you to Him. This little book is by no means the end all, be all about relationship to God. It is intended to be more or less an introduction by practical means to those who may have been "put off" by religion or anything to do with God because of some idiots who may have been well intentioned but nonetheless gave you the wrong idea of God. So, I want you to do this. I want you to get a copy of one of the Gospels in the New Testament of the Bible and read it. You know the ones, Matthew, Mark, Luke, or John, they are all known as the "Gospels" or "Good News" and in fact they are. My favourite is the Gospel of John, but they all tell about the life of Jesus of Nazareth. What I want to do is to give you the tools you need to make the choice to know God and love Him back; it really is as simple as that. And although you will certainly read a lot in this book that is detailed and may seem complicated, if you stick with me to the end you will find out in fact that God's plan has always been about us and Him. Through all of the complicated planning and detailed decision making, the simple message is that He created us because He wanted us, He loves us, and He wants us to choose to love Him back. The simplicity of God fits into one word and that word is the most amazing word mankind will ever know, and yet it is so simple. It is a name… Jesus.

He who does not love does not know God, for God is love.

1 John 4:8

1 The Short Version

I come before you now with a humble heart. It has taken a long time for me to come to this place because I am an arrogant, selfish, spoiled person. I believed that I have something new and inspiring to offer the world through my intelligence and study of God, only to realize that there is nothing I can tell you in this book that you cannot find many times over in books that have been written far better, grammatically correct, proper punctuation etc. . It's taken me years of compiling this book to finally realize the only difference that I can offer is my witness. What I have learned about and from God details the love story of how I came to have a relationship with the God of the Universe.

That love encompasses so very much especially for the young. Sad to say, but it really is true that the older we get the slimmer the chances of us getting to know God personally become. I think it's because life is hard and we learn to depend upon ourselves and our abilities which is good, don't misunderstand me, but we fail to pursue God who is greater than we are with a better plan in mind for us. It's the "abundant" life that Jesus taught that we tend to miss out on because of our pride or skepticism.

"The thief does not come except to steal, and to kill, and to destroy. I have come that they may have life, and that they may have it more abundantly." John 10:10 (NKJJV)

It has been my experience as a Born-Again Believer in Jesus since the age of nine to have benefitted from the abundance about which Jesus taught and the lack thereof when I depended solely upon myself. I am not referring to physical abundance as in riches and earthly possessions which will one day pass away. I am talking about peace and joy that reaches the depths of my innermost being that fulfills me in ways no earthly possession ever can or will.

So that will be the main difference between this book and other "religious" books other than this term that you will see many times throughout. Religion is man-made, Relationship is God made. Every other religion in the world demands that you do something to earn God's favor to be deserving of Heaven or an afterlife. Christianity says that God had done everything in order for you to have an eternal relationship with Him all you must do is believe it and receive it. So, before I detail my particular and unique story about how I came to know God we need to establish some things first. I believe if you will stick with me you will learn a lot and hopefully relate to some of the things that I have experienced and know that God is not only real but that He cares deeply about you and me and wants us to share our lives with Him. So here goes.

I am going to give you a very shortened version of what this little book contains. You may not be able to comprehend it all now but if you will continue to read these things will be discussed at length later.

There is only one True God. He is a Trinity or a Tri-unity meaning three in one. He consists of three distinct persons that are eternally interconnected. He consists of God the Father, God the Son also known as Jesus, and God the Holy Spirit. God is eternal meaning there is no beginning or end to Him. He is omnipotent meaning all powerful, omniscient meaning all knowing, omnipresent meaning everywhere, and above all He is Sovereign for there is nothing or no one above Him and His power. God is love, not simply described as a loving God but literally is love. This is the essence of His character which is unchanging. He once again is eternal, no beginning and no ending similar to a ring or a circle.

The God in three Persons known as the Trinity each have particular aspects to their personalities. God the Father is seated on His throne in Heaven, He is spirit with no physical aspect to Him. Jesus is seated at His right hand. He is the physical aspect of God. He is the one person of the God Head who spoke the Universe into existence, He is the One who determined before creation that He would become a man, come to earth, live a sinless life, die on a cross for the sins of the world, defeat death and be resurrected to prove to mankind that He was in fact God come to earth. He ascended back into Heaven after He had accomplished this and sent the third Person of the God Head, God the Holy Spirit to earth to help us regain our relationship with God the Father. The Person of the Holy Spirit is also the aspect of God that is omnipresent. He is in the world convicting mankind of their need for forgiveness of sin that has separated us from God.

God has a perfect plan for all of creation with its focus being that of mankind, His greatest love and creation. This plan began with the creation of Angels that are organized into a government of Angels meaning there are ranks of power and responsibility of these beings that God determined before the Universe was created. They serve God and do His will in Heaven. They worship Him and fulfill all of their duties willingly and with free will to do so as they were created directly by God. They are known as the Sons of God because they were directly created by Him. They have the power of free will given to them by God whereas they may choose to worship and obey Him or reject and rebel against Him. And this also is a direct result of the character of God who is love. Without choice there is no love. At the top of the ranks of Angels was an angel called Lucifer known as the "morning star".

The reason we know the Angels were created before the Universe is because the Bible tells us that they were there and saw it and "cheered" so to speak.

"When the morning stars sang together,

And all the sons of God shouted for joy?" Job 38:7
(NKJV)

The next thing God created was time. Time is a physical
dimension that was created to give mankind boundaries in
which to exist. God is outside of this dimension, however,
has the power to enter into or effect time according to His
will. The Angels were given the power to cross over the
dimension of time also as they would be used to assist
mankind.

The next thing God created was the Universe or as the
Bible tells us the Heavens and the Earth. This was of course
"the beginning" as time had been created.

"In the beginning God created the heavens and the
earth." Genesis 1:1 (NKJV)

You can read in the first chapter of Genesis the creation
of everything in the Universe with the Earth and everything
that is in it being the centerpiece of creation. And after
everything was perfectly created and prepared for the
pinnacle of His creation, mankind, God created man in His
own image. Adam and Eve are also known as son and
daughter of God because they were directly created by Him.
We on the other hand are sons and daughters of Adam as we
have been created through procreation, not directly by God.

When God created mankind, He choose to give us free
will. Once again without choice there is no true love. The

choices we make have consequences. And these consequences may be good or bad dependent upon what we choose. After all, it is our choice.

God created the earth and placed it in the perfect spot in the Universe, our solar system, for the atmosphere and gravity etc. He filled it with plants and animals, and then when it was perfectly prepared, He created man in His image and likeness and placed him in charge of the whole place. After God created man and placed him in such a high position with dominion over the earth and all its creatures, this apparently angered Lucifer. He had become so enamored with his intelligence, beauty, power and position that he desired to become God himself. This was when the first sin of pride occurred. The Bible tells us that "iniquity" was found in Lucifer and he was cast out of Heaven to the earth. Lucifer was then known as Satan meaning "adversary" and his thoughts and plans against God multiplied as the evil that now possessed him grew. Imagine him thinking, "What the heck is this? You created this puny little being made out of dust and you give HIM dominion over this amazing creation called earth and everything in it?" And this is when evil was exposed, the opposite of the Holy and perfect loving God. Lucifer was filled with pride and jealousy because he realized that he was not the apple of God's eye any longer. So, he rebelled against God and determined that he would be God now. Remember, he was created by God and he knew it, but because of his pride and jealousy he was blinded by this fact and truly believed that he could take God's place.

Not only did he announce that he was going to be like the Most High but he convinced a third of the angels to follow him in his quest to do so. So, understand this, Lucifer, no longer the "morning star" the highest angel, is now called Satan, which means the accuser along with many other descriptions through scripture such as the father of lies. And he sets his sights on the apple of God's eye, His most cherished creation, us, mankind.

"How you are fallen from heaven, O Lucifer, son of the morning! How you are cut down to the ground, you who weakened the nations! For you have said in your heart: 'I will ascend into heaven, I will exalt my throne above the stars of God; I will also sit on the mount of the congregation On the farthest sides of the North; I will ascend above the heights of the clouds, I will be like the Most High.'" Isaiah 14:12-14 (NKJV)

Satan knows the value God places on mankind and through his evil desires he himself planned a way in which to separate God from mankind. He knew that if he could get man to disobey God as he had done that this would destroy the relationship that man enjoyed with God so he set out to do just that. He approached Eve in the Garden and deceived her into disobeying God with Adam also following along.

This was the first sin committed by mankind that brought sin into all of creation.

Almost everyone has heard the story of Adam and Eve in the Garden of Eden but just in case I will give the short version. God creates Adam out of the dust of the ground, plants a garden in Eden for Adam to tend and places him there. God warns Adam not to eat from the tree in the middle of the garden, the tree of the knowledge of good and evil or he would die. Then God says that it is not good for man to be alone so he causes Adam to fall asleep and takes one of his ribs and forms a woman. Then one day Satan approaches the woman in the garden in the form of a serpent. The serpent deceives her and talks her into disobeying God and she eats of the tree of the knowledge of good and evil, gives some to Adam and it has been all downhill from there. God said; "what did you do"? Adam blamed Eve, Eve blamed the serpent and all of them were cursed and God kicked Adam and Eve out of the Garden and death and decay entered into the Universe because of sin. And that's where the separation between mankind and God began. Because of man's disobedience, sin, we became separated in our relationship to Him.

Now this pleased Satan greatly because he wanted to hurt God and do as much damage to Him and His prize creation as possible and what better way than to make it so that all communication with Him was cut off? Now that is what Satan was thinking. Remember, Satan is not God, and yet Satan is given power. In fact, the Bible teaches us that as a result of the "fall of man" Satan was given power over the earth, he becomes the prince of this world.

Now I am giving all of this information in a short version to bring us to the point that truly affects our lives today. Yes, all of the history of mankind is important, all of the stories in the Bible, the witnesses of others even alive today are relevant but what it all boils down to is what you believe in your heart. First the recognition of God has to be there. Just the simple agreement that there is a God and He created everything. If you agree to this then you must rationally agree that He has laws or rules upon which this universe operates. Without rules there is chaos. But let's pause and look at the whole thing the way I believe God does. He didn't create the universe, all the planets, the solar system, the earth and everything that is in it, and place mankind in it just for fun. God doesn't do anything without perfect purpose. He doesn't guess, or wonder, or imagine because He already knows the outcome before He sets anything in motion. This is difficult for our minds to comprehend but I am asking you to try. You see, the whole reason for all of creation was us. You, me, and all of the billions of people who have lived over time since the creation of the world. We are the focus of all of creation because He wants to have a relationship with each one of us individually, but by choice. He wants us to choose Him back.

But He also had more to His plan. I mean seriously, God does not need Angels to worship Him 24/7 although He

9

certainly deserves to be worshipped and adored, after all He IS God! His plan included something more near and dear to His heart. Us! His plan has ALWAYS been about US! He knew that He would be creating us and that we would have a choice to make. Now remember, God is Holy and Perfect! He did not create evil, but understand that the absence of good leaves room for evil to flourish. Satan is the one who determined to look at God and His holiness and rebel and reject it and determine to do the exact opposite of God.

Ok then you ask the question well then why did God create Satan if He is all knowing and knew Satan would become who he is? Good question and I will attempt to answer it. The Bible tells us that when Satan rejected God a third of the created angels also did the same and followed Satan. These are known as fallen angels also known as demons. These are created beings that were also given choice and chose to rebel against their creator and follow a liar known as Satan. However, there are still two-thirds that chose to remain and obey their creator and worship and serve Him. So, the answer I believe is that God created the angels for man. You see He knew that man would be in need of the assistance of angels because of the spiritual battle that man would face as a result of sin. Yes, He knew that one-third would reject Him and disobey Him and yet He was willing to suffer this because of the ultimate outcome.

God created Satan fully aware that he would eventually reject Him and seek to rule in His place. Evil began with Satan. Sin is our choice to reject God. Our ancestors all the way back to Adam and Eve chose to sin; Simple as that. Sin entered the world by choice and it has been the reason our relationship to God has been so hard.

Beloved if God so loved us, we also ought to love one another.

1 John 4:11

2 Why Me? Why Now?

I have struggled with this little book for several years. I have come into contact with and known countless people with whom I have desired to share my story but because of time constraints or circumstances beyond my control, I missed that opportunity. Perhaps it was just my own unwillingness or laziness, regardless, I wanted to have something that I could give to someone that would give them opportunity to know what I know. When you know God it's like having the cure to the world's diseases and keeping it to yourself if you don't share it. The problem for us today is that we have been so intimidated by the world that we tend to hold onto this precious knowledge for ourselves, spend time with others like ourselves, and rarely if ever share this magnificent gift. In this world today there is so much controversy, so many different points of view, so many religions that it is easy to understand how many are confused as to how they can know God. Let me suggest to you that these many religions and points of view are manmade. God's way is relationship, not religion.

Consider that God is reaching out to you in this fashion perhaps because He will be able to reach you through an imperfect person like myself. What I tell you I believe with my whole heart. I may come from a different background than you, I am certain we have different life experiences and perhaps world views, however we have the most important attribute in common; our ability to choose. I am asking you to choose to hear me out. Listen to what I have to say and then make your choice. It is after all a decision that is between you and God alone. If you want to know God, I can tell you how. I cannot however tell you what His particular plan for your life is. I firmly believe that He has one, beginning right now your life can change and your future along with it, and it all depends on your choice.

Writing a book is no easy task I have discovered. There are so many aspects to consider. Of course, the author, me in this case, has a desire to share a specific amount of information whether it be for entertainment or education, in a manner that satisfies the reader. Actually, the author desires that the reader really like his or her finished product. The key word here is desire. Unfortunately, this is not always the case but I am optimistic and hope that you will find that my desire and your experience are one and the same. Although I do not wish for you to consider this an arrogant mentality. I fully expect that what is contained in this book will be controversial for a few, rejected by some, and embraced by others. The hope is that you will read what I share with an open heart and mind, with a willingness to benefit from it. I believe it is a choice, your choice.

The problem I have had since the inception of this book is how to come across to the reader (you) in a way that is appealing and interesting. Publishers want the book to sell and make their company money. I certainly would like to make some money also but understand this first and foremost. I am not writing this book for money, that in all honesty is a small part of it. I abhor the idea of anyone getting rich off of their religion, ESPECIALLY Christians. The main reason I am writing this book is because I have the love of God in me and it is overflowing. And yet I am angry. I am angry at the enemy of God's creation who seeks to destroy us and keep us from a relationship with God. His name was Lucifer (Morning Star) and now is Satan (Adversary/Accuser). I am tired of him lying and deceiving the people God loves and watching them over and over blame God for circumstances caused by the influence of Satan. First, we must KNOW God and then TRUST Him to help us fight against this evil. We must be proactive in our lives and not just reactive!

So how does being angry go hand in hand with telling about God's love? You must know that we are in a daily battle. You have to sense it. Everyday there is a battle against something or someone that you didn't expect or understand where it began. The Bible calls this "spiritual warfare". We are spirit beings living in flesh bodies. Our spirits, or the essence of the individuals that we are, are like the software on a computer. Our spirits are the software and our bodies are the hardware. One day this hardware will break down and perish, but our software, our spirit, will live on. Where will it go? That is up to us and our decisions. I don't know any other way than to tell you the truth and you make the choice of whether or not to believe it. The choice is yours. Choice is one of the greatest gifts God has given to mankind, and the reason is that He would rather us choose to love Him and not be forced to. He didn't create us as a bunch of mindless robots, puppets on strings. No! He created us with free will, reasoning power, CHOICE! Understand that you have the responsibility to learn and educate yourself about any given topic. If you want to know the truth you can. It is out there. It is in this little book. It is ultimately up to you. What do you choose?

But the title of this book is "Because I Love You; The Simplicity of God." True love is just that, TRUE. So, it is imperative that someone, hopefully a lot of someone's start telling the TRUTH without fear of offending. And these days there is always the risk of offending. It seems no matter what we do, think, or say someone is looking to be offended. We live in a screwed-up world these days where left is right and right is wrong and people are losing hope and becoming apathetic because they don't know THE TRUTH. God is love and His truth is the only truth that matters. I am not God and neither are you and when we come to realize this and act accordingly then we have the chance to be victorious against the evil that is determined to destroy us. I can spend a lot of time defending myself, explaining myself, and hope that you understand me, however, that is not my job. My job and purpose is to point YOU in the direction of THE God who loves you. It is all about you and Him. I already have a relationship with Him, and as imperfect as I am, He still loves, comforts, protects, provides, strengthens, and encourages me, and I want the same for you.

The title of this book really is descriptive of myself as well as God. You see, believe it or not I do love you. Although I may not know you or ever meet you, my heart has a longing for you to have something that I have that is the most valuable possession known to man; knowing God; THE GOD. Now pay close attention to that terminology; KNOWING God, not knowing ABOUT God, there is a huge difference. That is not intended to be self-righteous or condescending as I am no more or less important to God than you and I want you do discover this for yourself as I have. God has brought me to this point right now as I am writing with the realization that whatever you gain from this little book is going to be up to you and Him, your willingness to learn and act upon it has to be your choice and dependent upon you, not me.

I am a man, 59 years old. I am the husband of a wonderful, loving, caring, talented woman who I don't deserve but am happy to claim. I am also the father of two beautiful teenage daughters that we were blessed to bring into our family from the People's Republic of

China. I know, God has a sense of humor doesn't He, me a dad to two teenagers at 59 years of age. Perhaps that is why my faith is so strong. I was born and raised in Columbia, South Carolina in the United States of America. Interestingly enough this area is considered a part of the "Bible Belt" and I am the beneficiary of growing up there. Although I was raised in a "Christian" home and learned quite a bit about God through this point of view, I certainly made the choice in my life to branch out and discover different "Faiths" or "Religions". So please don't pigeon hole me as just a Southerner with a radical fundamental Christian view. I believe you will find that although I label myself "Christian" and I don't necessarily like labels, I am not someone who has blindly followed a "religion" all of my life; no, quite the contrary. I have discovered over the years that religions are man-made, relationship is God made. What I mean is, man has continued to reach out to God desiring to please Him and benefit from the act of "pleasing" him; i.e. gaining a place in heaven, or the "afterlife".

In this age of "political correctness" everyone has been cowered into a fear of offending anyone about anything. Some would rather have us ignorant regarding our beliefs. Who was it that said; "knowledge is power"? By keeping people scared of speaking to each other out of fear, the majority of folk simply would rather keep to themselves and to others like them. You know the saying, "Birds of a feather flock together". The problem is that there is so much to be learned from others, as well as to be taught by each of us that we are truly missing out on so much. We all have our life stories, our worldview, and although each one is unique, there is so much more that we have in common than upon which we disagree.

So why is it then that we seem to have so much difficulty sharing our religious beliefs with those about which we care? It seems reasonable to me that if you have a belief system you believe to be superior to others you would be willing to freely share this information. If you bought a great car, you couldn't wait to share that information with others, all of its bells and whistles, etc. How about a new recipe? My wife got our family an instant pot last year and has been singing its praises to everyone. In fact, we all love it so much that I will text her recipes I come across on social media! We want others to succeed, to share in the joy of the experience of something superior. (short definition of superior; 1-of high standard or quality. (dictionary.com)

But what happens when two people share their beliefs with each other and they disagree? One of two things happen. They are mature enough to accept and respect the others beliefs and continue to go on with their relationship, or they childishly (immaturely) determine that they can no longer have a relationship with that person because their beliefs are not the same. And I might add that it has been my experience that those who choose to end a relationship based upon differing beliefs aren't really that convinced that their beliefs are correct, they just have taken a stand and won't deter from it regardless of other options afforded to them.

But don't people know that your faith is personal? Don't they know the old adage that you don't talk religion, politics and sex with friends and coworkers? By the way, from where did that old adage originate? When was the last time you got really angry at a friend who recommended a restaurant or movie? Seriously, even if the restaurant wasn't that great or the movie was just "so-so" you didn't go and give them a piece of your mind in an angry fashion did you? I hope not, after all they were simply wanting to share their experience with you, someone they apparently care about. And I am sure that if the restaurant was exceptional and the movie was outstanding you were very happy to thank your friend for recommending them to you and also share your experience with others. What I am sharing with you is so much more than a recommendation of a place to eat or some form of entertainment. It is eternally consequential.

You have to believe something. Perhaps you aren't sure exactly what you believe. Maybe you already disagree with my statement that you have to believe something. But just think about that. Disagreeing with it means that you believe it to be wrong. Therefore, you must believe something. I am writing this for you who want answers. First, I will tell you that I do not have all the answers to your questions, but it is my intention to point you to someone who does have all the answers. That person is the one true God who loves you, created you, and has a plan for your life. Most importantly, it is your choice as whether or not you respond to His calling to you. He knows you better than you know yourself. He created you and wants you to know Him as intimately as He knows you, but once again, the choice is yours. What will you choose?

Perhaps you are saying to yourself right now; "great, another religious pitch about god, another dead end, another unkept promise. I don't buy into all that religious crap that the millionaire televangelists spout on television, all the 'feel good' god is 'Santa Claus' and will give you everything you ask for. In fact, I am so sick of organized religion that I could puke, so please don't pull that crap with me!" And I couldn't agree with you more because I can relate, to some degree, where you get this attitude. Even with the best intentions man has screwed up religion, especially the Christian religion, with his own answers instead of God's answers. So, let's make an agreement right now before we go any further so you can know what you may be getting yourself into. I am not the focus of this book, you are. Hopefully it is your desire to have a relationship with THE GOD, not a pretender, or your idea of who He is, or someone else's either, but THE ONE TRUE GOD. And I know God wants you to experience this personal relationship with Him because He loves you and created you. So, understand that this is a journey about you and Him, I am just the messenger.

The reason I am telling you this is that I want you to consider me a straightforward man with a simple desire. Perhaps not simple, but not arrogantly complicated either. The desire of which I speak is to share how and why to do the single most important thing that you can do in your life, establish a relationship with God. Let me clarify this because of its importance; THE GOD, not a god, or who you believe god to be, or who you imagine god is. I don't wish to attempt to impress you with a lot of socially approved accomplishments that would in turn give you a reason to give validity to what I write. No, I think the reason that God has given me the desire to do this is because I am not "qualified" in a worldly mind set. And this is fitting because the purpose of this book is for you to be the one that is qualified. You are the one who will decide whether what I am sharing with you is worth considering and acting upon or not. The whole point is that it's about you and your choices. Connecting with God is not about knowing the right prayer or visiting the right priest/preacher. It's not about what building you walk into, what songs you sing, any particular dance, chant, candle you light, how many times a day you pray, etc. It's about the condition of your heart. What is your heart's desire? The Bible tells us;

"For man looks at the outward appearance, but the LORD looks at the heart."

I Samuel 16:7(NKJV)

God is concerned with your heart and truly only you and God know what is in your heart. Regarding this I am reminded of my Grandfathers admonition; "I can fool you, and you can fool me. But you can't fool God". My Grandfather was a wise man.

We all want answers. The longer you live the more questions you have. And as you grow older you discover that there doesn't seem to be sufficient answers to some of life's biggest questions. And sometimes we find that the answers we get aren't always right, or complete. So, we accept what seems reasonable to us and adjust our beliefs based upon the information we obtain as time goes on. This is why we consider older people to be wiser people. Having more life experiences tends to make a person wiser simply by the record of failure and success. We tend to learn a great deal more from our failures than our successes. I should be a genius by now according to this opinion. I have failed a lot over the course of my lifetime, or have I? Truly failure is giving up isn't it? Then I will consider my life a series of delayed successes. Perhaps you should consider yours this way also. After all, why are you reading this book? Are you looking for answers? I hope so because it will be full of them. But be forewarned that the answers may be here, what you do with the information you receive is your responsibility.

I believe I told you in the introduction that this was not a religious book, or at least I don't want it to be considered as such. It is my opinion that religion(s) have gotten a bad reputation over the years for good reason, they can be corrupt and full of deception. I want you to consider this book to be more of a "self-help spiritual" book of sorts,

if that makes sense. In other words, it is a book that will give you information to help yourself spiritually which is what is the most important ambition of my writing this to you. I believe that God is more concerned with our spirituality than anything else. Now having

said this I may sound hypocritical in stating that although I don't want

this to be a religious book for stated reasons, I must examine religion in order to make the points needed to be made. In short, I know that there is a religion that is the right one, the one that God wants us to follow. Now I know that sounds arrogant but hear me out.

Now to some of you that won't make a lot of sense, to others it will be offensive or crazy and that is fine because many of you subscribe to a religion that may teach something different. To that I say this statement and you will see it again several times in this book. Religion is manmade Relationship is God made.

I am going to ask you to be totally honest with yourself when you approach what I have written in this book. This is going to be a journey between you and God. You are going to have to answer the questions as to what you truly believe and why. Are you frustrated with your faith? Do you tend to worship your beliefs more than the One in whom you believe? What I mean is that it is human nature to glorify "things" so that we being a part of these "things" feel more important or "validated". Why else would we feel the need to dress fashionably, or go to the most popular restaurants, or read the "right" books? Why so many seek fame and adoration from others? We long for others to recognize our value, that we have a purpose, a reason for being alive on this planet.

Perhaps you have simply rejected organized religion in any form and determined for yourself what you deem appropriate regarding a "higher power". How is that working out for you? Being honest with ourselves is one of the most difficult challenging undertakings. Recognizing our strengths and weaknesses is sometimes a battle. But in order to benefit from this self-awareness we must be willing to engage in change. And for us humans change itself can cause discomfort and fear. But that is a decision for you and God to make. Do you need to make a change? What would that look like? What exactly are you looking FOR?

There was a religious song that was popular a few years ago, "There's a God shaped hole in all of us" was either it's title or hook. Regardless the point is that it is a true statement. Even the Atheist who will deny that there is a God has simply hardened their heart to the truth of this. The sad aspect for so many today is that they attempt to fill this hole with religion and it doesn't work out. The reason being is that Religion is man-made and Relationship is God made. In other words, God's purpose in creating all of us is that He desires a personal relationship with each one of us, individually. He being our creator already knows us better than we know ourselves so this relationship requires us to work on knowing Him. Not simply knowing about Him, not going through all of the religious motions of whatever religion to which you subscribe, but literally KNOWING Him. A relationship requires that both parties be involved and both actively so.

I can attest to this, as so many like myself also can. But in truth, all I can do is share with you what I have found to be true. What my relationship with God has been like and how and why I believe it is true with every fiber of my being. And once again, I am not alone in this as there are literally millions of others who have a personal relationship with God because they were willing to do one simple thing; Believe. Believe that it is possible to have a close personal relationship with the God who created everything. Believe that He is a loving God and that His love is so great that it is a natural outpouring of this love that He desires this relationship with us. Believe that His love looks beyond who we are and what we have done, good and bad, and loves us just because.

One of the biggest hurdles many have to negotiate is recognizing their importance in Gods view. In other words, we tend to rationalize to ourselves that God cannot simply care about me in an up close and personal way as there are billions of people on the planet and He can't take the time to just be concerned with me. However, in doing this we are limiting the all-powerful, all knowing, loving God. Take a moment and think about how this Universe and all that is within it even exists. Do you believe that we live on a planet that is perfectly positioned in this solar system, perfect gravitation, air, water, food sources, etc. by chance? Even considering evolution, the odds of this occurring are astronomical, quite frankly absurd, and yet there are those who would rather believe this than place their faith in God. And yet if you believe in God and yet deny His power to know you intimately and desire for you to know Him likewise, are you no different in your thinking? Isn't it absurd to limit God?!

So, once again I am reminding you to challenge yourself. Be totally honest and attempt an understanding of what it is that you believe and why. If you don't have a good enough "why" then perhaps it is because you haven't given God the opportunity to help you with that. Notice how I didn't say given man the opportunity to help you with that. I understand that this sounds a little hypocritical because it is a man writing this book, sharing this information with you. But understand this, my efforts in writing this book are for the purpose of pointing you to God, not me. It is the testimony of my relationship to God and my earnest desire for you to have one also.

And allow me to be blunt; you need a personal relationship with God, He doesn't need one with you; more importantly, He DESIRES one with you. The God who created the Universe and all that is within it desires for you to know Him intimately for the purpose of an eternal relationship. Don't limit God. Don't believe that He doesn't care about every aspect of your life. The Bible tells us;

"But the very hairs of your head are all numbered." Matthew 10:30 (NKJV)

This means that God knows how many hairs you have on your head, and in my case that is not a whole lot, but more importantly He has assigned a specific number to each hair. This is significant because it is meant to show us the intricate detail of our lives of which He is aware. So why would He not care about the smallest concern of yours? If we are being honest with ourselves, perhaps the reason we shy away from the intimate relationship with God is because we want to deny that He knows everything about us already, intimately. And this would include our thoughts. Uh oh, I felt that one too. But don't be afraid of that fact because I can tell you from personal experience that God loves us in spite of our thoughts and actions. And perhaps most importantly of all is the understanding that we cannot disappoint God because He knows what we are going to do even before we do it! But don't be deceived, we can certainly disappoint ourselves and others and be ashamed of ourselves and feel guilty. Yes, shame and guilt are vitally important if we are to truly seek God. We must recognize our need for His forgiveness. This is a concept that is not a popular one in today's politically correct environment and perhaps one of the reasons that so many bad things are escalating in our world.

There is a way that seems right to a man,

but its end is the way of death. Proverbs 14:12

3 Truth or Consequences

Humanity is in trouble. This is nothing new, we have been in trouble since we chose to rebel from God and chose our own path. This is known as sin; and as a result of sin we have all of the problems in the world today. All of our choices are influenced as a result of sin and most importantly sin caused and still causes a separation from God. Because of sin we no longer have the intimate personal relationship with God that He wanted for us from the beginning. But there is hope. And that hope is in the person of Jesus Christ. Two thousand years ago, a man claiming to be God incarnate died a horrible death on a cross. He was raised from the dead on the third day and proved to the world that He was God in the flesh. He did all of this so that we could once again have that intimate relationship with God that we had at creation. He did it so that we could be forgiven of the sins that separated us from God. And He did it freely because of His great love for us. All we have to do is receive His gift to us by faith and we can have that relationship with God forever. And there it is again folks; I invoked the G word. God with a capital G. You did read the title of the book, right? Because I love You, the simplicity of God. Should have been a clue that I would be talking about God but for some of you out there who chose to be fence straddlers i.e. Agnostics, or even the die-hard Atheists I will be more than happy to debate reasonably God's existence. And in great company I might add, after all there are literally billions of people living today who believe in some form of God, or "higher power". Even the scientific community has determined a phrase acceptable to their standards: Remember the term "the uncaused cause?" Yeah, try and figure that one out. There is something that caused everything to be here in existence and it was uncaused. In other words, they won't acknowledge God, or any higher power other than calling whatever it is as "uncaused" which means that scientifically they don't have answers.

It's as if we are riding on a carousel that is sitting on a big flatbed truck traveling at a high rate of speed towards a cliff, and no one seems to notice or care because we are all reaching for the brass ring that will give us another free ride. Expectations for ourselves and others are so often unrealistic and unattainable that we allow meaningless distractions to appease our desire to achieve meaningful results. The consequence being a continual vicious cycle of disappointment and frustration that ultimately leads to more distractions and finally hopelessness. If you don't agree or believe me, I encourage you to just look around you, your friends, loved ones, acquaintances. How many are addicted to something? It may be their phone, politics, sex, or drugs. Addiction generally follows hopelessness like a puppy following a child home. Addiction begins out of a need to distract ourselves from some part of our reality that we do not like and cannot control. You know what I am talking about. We all know people who are obsessed with social media, those who are fixated on politics, others who are passionately dedicated to their religion, and of course the slave of workaholism. All of these distractions do one thing perfectly well, they keep us so busy that we don't take the time to be still and focus on what is the most important aspect of our lives; Relationships.

When I first conceived of writing this book, I was overwhelmed at the prospect of trying to communicate all of my thoughts and desires in a clear concise manner. I have such a passion for others to know what I know and I don't say that arrogantly, I am just like someone who experiences a great meal at a restaurant and can't wait to share my experience with others. However, this information is so far beyond an opinion about an eating establishment. This information effects lives now and eternally. But as I have battled the writing of this book, deciding on what to say where, how to say it, pondering what would be the possible response to any given issue, I finally came to what I had been looking for. Amazing as it is, I began this project with simplicity in mind. I wanted to share the simplicity of God and how He loves us. And in this well intended process I lost my simplicity. I lost the fact that it is not my job to convince you of anything. You are going to believe what you choose to believe based upon you. I am a messenger and am going to tell you things and you will have to believe them or not based upon you. I know God is working on getting you to the truth if that is what you desire. It's going to have to be your work, you going to God and asking Him if what I say in this book is true. It really is that simple. It's all about choice, and the choice is yours alone.

I am not hopeless; I am full of hope and enthusiasm for what I have experienced in this life with anticipation for the life to come. I know I was created by a loving, all powerful God, who has a purpose for not only me but all of mankind. I was not just some fluke of nature, there is way too much scientific evidence that backs up an intelligent design for our universe. I know what I believe and why I believe it. I believe in God, not just any god but THE GOD; The God of Abraham, Isaac, and Jacob spoken of in the Holy Bible. Not just because it's the socially acceptable thing, to believe in

God, but because I have a personal relationship with Him. I KNOW Him and more importantly He knows me. He has a plan for my life because He designed and planned me. Just as you were designed and planned also. And one of the greatest gifts He gave to us besides the gift of life, is the gift to choose. He gives us the right to choose what we will do, how we will think, etc. And this is simply because God is Love. He wants us to choose to love Him back, not be forced to. Would you rather have someone choose to love you or be forced to? And so, it is with God, he didn't create us as puppets on strings so He could be the puppet master. He gives us choice.

And choosing to have a relationship with God is a beautiful, amazing, supernatural thing. I mean we are talking about God, the all-knowing, all powerful, God. And what amazes me even more is that every person's relationship with God is different and yet so similar. What I mean is that we are all created similarly, physically, meaning we all bleed red blood and breathe oxygen. We all have basic human needs and desires so we have similarities in this way. And yet we all are unique because we are all individuals with a soul, the eternal aspect of who we were created to be. And our souls are attached to our spirit which is the life force given to us by God. Better described and understood in this day and age as "software". Our souls are the unique individual aspects of who we are connected to the life or spirit given to us by God. We reside in a "hardware" body, but our software is constantly being upgraded and improved as we grow. So, having a relationship with the programmer would seem like a good idea if you ask me. Especially since we live in a world with corrupted codes and viruses and malware. We need protection and a relationship with God gives us that and the ability to live out our lives to the best of our abilities with the assistance of an amazing programmer. Wow, that was a pretty cool analogy if you ask me and I am not a computer nerd!

But here's the catch; You can't have a personal relationship with God without help. You see sin, that's transgression against Gods law, (following the previously mentioned analogy it could be considered a lethal virus) has separated us from Him and there must be payment (anti-virus) for sin. The Bible tells us;

"For all have sinned and fall short of the glory of God." Romans 3:23 (NKJV) It also tells us "For the wages of sin is death, but the gift of God is eternal life in Jesus Christ our Lord". Romans 6:23 (NKJV)

So according to the Bible, we all have sinned and earned death as a result but then there's the Jesus statement. Eternal life in Jesus, how does that work? Jesus is basically the ultimate anti-virus. According to the Bible, which is God's word and a message system by which we can live our lives, Jesus is God in the flesh. In other words, God became flesh so that He could teach us the will of God the Father.

Now of course I found this out through my relationship first and foremost with my parents. The first relationship that I had. My mother and father had a relationship with God and wanted me to have the same. First, I had to know about God. That's where the religion part came in. I was raised in a Christian home environment. I should call it a God relationship environment. Because it wasn't just about following the belief system of a religion and all of its guidelines, it was first and foremost KNOWING God in a way that He gave me direction through all of the "guidelines". Does that make sense? Yeah, I know, bad title calling it the simplicity of God huh? But the truth is that it is simple. We have a tendency to make it complicated.

I was raised as a Christian. Let's dig a little deeper into that label and let me explain what that should mean. I say, should, because through the years that label has been used and abused by well-intentioned as well as ill-intentioned people. Being a Christian should mean a follower, or believer in Jesus the Christ, or as many say, "Jesus Christ". The Christ part comes from the Greek meaning "Messiah". So, when someone says they are a Christian they should mean that they believe in Jesus as the Messiah or "Christ". Yeah, I know, getting seriously religious sounding but understand this. The reason that religion or "religious talk" confuses or sometimes offends people is because of the multitudes of Religions that are out there. So many that offer their idea of who God is and what He is about. And more or less what you have to do or become or believe to find your way to God.

Perhaps you know this or have heard it before but just bear with me as I am desiring to help those who may not have heard it, or simply have never understood it to do so. I think the reason that so many people are "put off" by religions and avoid the topic altogether is that they find it too complicated. That is why it is important to understand that God's plan has always been simple, not complicated. In its truest form, a relationship with God is simple. Living life is complicated, understanding, or should I say, trying to understand God is complicated. That is, without a personal relationship with Him is next to impossible. Doesn't it make sense that so many just choose to avoid it altogether? Well, there is a reason for that. Someone does not want you to know God, much less have a relationship with Him. And here it comes.... The person named, yep you have heard it before, Satan. The father of lies, the prince of darkness, the deceiver, you get the picture.

Like so many of you, I have lived through hell on earth many times and only survived by the grace and mercy of THE God whom I know loves us so well. I have seen so much pain and suffering. I have experienced the same and although there were times that I thought it was God who was responsible for my sufferings I came to know that this was not the case. Therefore, I know that whatever you are going through, whatever you have experienced in your life that I don't know about and may never know, God does. He wants a relationship with you because He loves you and knows you need Him. He doesn't need you, better yet, He WANTS you. So, bear with me, forgive my imperfection and read on and learn the simple truth of God, Because I Love you!

I am a very small part of this world. It is a great big world with so many different places, faces, cultures, belief systems, etc. I have had to question myself so many times how I have the audacity to think that I have something important to say to the world and I realized that I truly was being extremely arrogant in thinking that I do. I had to come to the realization that for whatever purpose God has in inspiring me to write this, it's not my message that is the important one. And this message is the most important message for the whole world, but realistically I can only affect my little world for Him. I can be a part of that amazing message of how much He loves us and has done everything in His power to give us the choice to choose Him back, to love Him back. And this is the message of Jesus.

"Nor is there salvation in any other, for there is no other name under heaven, given among men by which we must be saved." Acts 4:12 (NKJV)

The best way for me to share this message with you is by the witness of my lifelong relationship with God through Jesus. I have to tell you about what I have learned personally through my relationship with God. I am not an expert in theology, or any religious field of study, however I am an expert in my relationship with the One and True God of the Universe. I have avoided focusing on me in the writing of this book because I didn't want it to be about me, rather I wanted to try and appeal to sensibilities and rational thought processes in order to convince you that what I believe is true. It's not as if this is a multi-level marketing company and the more people that I introduce to Jesus I get a waffle iron and move up in the company. It's more like I know the location of the tree that gives the fruit that when you eat of it, you are eternally cured and I want you to be cured because I have been cured and there is nothing like knowing that.

Sure, I would like to sell some books, I have two teenage daughters that will decide if college is in their future very soon and I would like to have the security of knowing that we don't have to struggle to pay those bills. Not to mention, did I say two daughters? Someday and probably sooner than later they will fall in love and want to get married and that is another cash outlay. So, being someone who lives on a meager income of disability and limited in physical ability I am doing what I can with the part of my body that still cooperates, my mind. If I sell a million copies then wonderful, if I sell only a few and those few introduce someone to Jesus then all of the effort will have been worth it.

The point is that we all have gifts that God has given to us that we should willingly share with others, and then we also will reap the benefits of their gifts that they share with us. My gift to you is my story, my witness of knowing this amazing God who loves us in ways we cannot imagine. He teaches us and leads us according to our willingness to obey and love Him back. The Bible tells us:

"the Lord is not slow about His promise as some count slowness, but is forbearing toward you, not wishing that any should perish, but that all should reach repentance." 2Peter 3:9 RSV

God does not desire for anyone to be eternally separated from Him and so He made the way for us to be together by the forgiveness of our sins through believing in His Son, Jesus. There is also that phrase that drives me crazy, although it is well intentioned by those who utter it. You may be one of those people so let me give you something to think about before you use it next time. The phrase is "everything happens for a reason". This really is a "cop out" phrase, perhaps meaning well, but what it does is tend to excuse the person from responsibility for their choices or the choices of others that have affected them and squarely puts it all on God's shoulders which is wrong.

We want an easy answer for everything, bad, good, or indifferent. We don't want to recognize that things happen due to our choices. Do you agree with the ignorance in that statement now? Everything happens as a result of choices made. Now perhaps they weren't necessarily your choices but the culmination of the choices that we as mankind have made. However, we must admit that our choices have the most effect on us and those around us. And choices have a trickle-down effect. For example, in the country of my birth, the United States of America, we are known as a Constitutional Republic or a Representative Democracy. Our government has established laws that are determined by the choices our Representatives make. They make choices about the laws they will establish. We as voters have determined who will be making these decisions. Our government has been established upon choices made years ago that affect our lives today.

There are no easy answers, simple yes, effortless no. The whole truth of The God is simple in its abstract, however the problem is that we tend to lean towards the complex believing it to be more valuable. The more we know about any given subject the smarter we believe ourselves to be. And in this mix of "self-awareness" we tend to lose sight of simplicity. This is the reason that Jesus taught us to come to Him as a little child, with childlike faith.

"But Jesus said, 'Let the little children come to Me, and do not forbid them; for of such is the kingdom of heaven.'" Matthew 19:14 (NKJV)

When we were small, we had certain people that we trusted and therefore we believed them. If they told us that up was really down and black was really white, we didn't doubt it because we had the simplistic faith to believe and trust. This is what is required for a relationship with God. You must believe and have faith. Straightforward, but not natural, especially in this day and age.

Throughout the world people are looking for answers. Some want answers to complex problems, others just want to know simple things. Complex; how was the universe created? Simple; why was I created? Most of us start out by looking for the answers to the simple. My goal was to start with foundational information and build upon it. Surely you noticed that you didn't find a lot of answers to complex scientific questions here especially nothing on math. I never even took chemistry in high school but I did enjoy biology. No, what I want to do is to give you tools with which to work. You will do the work because that is what God wants you to do. He wants you to use the mind He gave you, your reasoning power to determine whether or not what you have read and are reading here is true. I already know what I believe. And yes, I still have questions myself, but not for the simple stuff. I have gone down that road before and I will never take that path again.

What path is that? Glad you asked. It is the path to least resistance. The path that is full of lemmings that will go in which direction the flute player is directing. The Bible calls it the path to destruction and many are going and have gone that way. The path that leads to life, the truth, is a narrow path and you must be willing to step out in faith and trust to experience the truth.

"Enter by the narrow gate; for wide is the gate and broad is the way that leads to destruction and there are many who go in by it. Because narrow is the gate and difficult is the way which leads to life and there are few who find it." Matthew 7:13-14 (NKJV)

Remember how I stated earlier that truth is a subject many love to discuss as if it is a subjective thing. In reality truth is exactly what it says it is. It's not "my" truth or "your" truth, although you may hear people talk this way. Let me warn you that those that speak like this have no idea what real truth is. They are on the path to destruction because they are determining truth for themselves. And that is not THE truth. I know it sounds complex but really, it's not, it is simple. Jesus said that He was the truth, meaning that there is no lie or dishonesty about Him. You can bank on every word that He said. And understand this, many things He said may have multiple meanings or "layers" kind of like an onion. He spoke a lot in parables or little stories with simple meaning and as you uncover the layers you discover other possibilities. Now don't misunderstand what I am saying here.

The Good News of Jesus Christ has not changed, the world has. We live in a day and age where the truth of Jesus is still as relevant as it was two thousand years ago, even more so. However, the world is too distracted to hear it. The heart longs for it but the itching ears that long for something more temporal, more physically appealing wins out. This is why we must be willing to fight for the truth of who and what Jesus is. We have to love others enough to risk hurting ourselves in the process. What I mean is that we have to reach out beyond our everyday comfort zone and be willing to be thought the fool, offend others, and lose friends and acquaintances for the love of Jesus. We have to love them to Christ. I know that sounds foreign to those who of you who are not born-again believers, perhaps you are familiar with the saying; "they will know we are Christians by our love"? And when we think of love we think of the warm gushy feeling of happiness and security right? But doesn't your parent love you when they spank your hand away from the open flame? When they bust your behind for running out into the street without looking? How is this love? You know exactly what I mean by that, especially if you are a parent. You want the best for your children, and you are willing to have them cry and be mad at you for a while until they are old enough to understand your discipline. Then why should it not be the same with our Heavenly Father? Doesn't He have the right to bust our behinds when we are running out into the midst of something dangerous? Doesn't He have the right, better yet, the love, to spank our hands away from things that will hurt us?

How about this; Grandparents are most assuredly used by God with parent's approval and appreciation. They of course love to spoil their grandkids but they understand when enough is enough and most are not afraid to correct a grandchild when needed. God is willing and able to do the same through us. When He wants to make a point to us, teach us something, hasn't he used numerous people in your life? I believe that we live in the day and age where we have to allow Him to use us to speak the truth about Jesus boldly to others. We cannot permissibly sit by and allow our friends, family, coworkers, etc. to believe the cunning lies of Satan through all of the lying religions that deny the divinity of Jesus. Religions that deny that He is the ONLY way to know God, The One True Living God. How dare we say we love others and yet are willing to let them comfortably fall into an eternity without Him. Forget about Hell for right now. Yes, that is important enough. But have you been paying attention? The world we are living in now has become a type of Hell on earth. The decay of morals, corruption at the highest levels of every once respected institution, and yes, sadly to say, even leadership within the Church. This world needs Christ like perhaps never before in the history of mankind. We need Him because the world we are living in has lost hope and has blinders on.

You've heard it said, "No man is an island" well, we don't live on an island totally self-sufficient without the need of others. We require assistance whether we like it or not. And no one is independent, no one. Yes, someone may think that they are independent but that is simply an illusion. No matter where you live on this planet you require something from someone or something.

Let's say you are stranded on an island. You must have water, food and shelter to survive. Perhaps you have to build a shelter so that makes you feel good; you have provided for yourself. You have to have food and so you somehow catch fish or make a trap for small animals, build a fire and cook the food. You have done very well. And of course, you need fresh water because our bodies must have water or we will die. But there is no source of fresh water on the island, and then it begins to rain.

Let's say you live in New York City. You have a decent job that provides adequate income, and a reasonable place to live. You are a loner and don't need anyone, you are totally self-sufficient and independent. This is an illusion. First, you only have the job because someone in your business hired you. The business only exists because it has a product that someone needs and wishes to purchase. You have electricity because someone else has a job of making that electricity. You have food because someone grew it, or killed it, or processed it. Get the picture? The saying, "No man is an island," is true.

I am writing this book on a computer. Someone invented it, someone produced the many materials that went into the actual physical computer itself. And then someone had to design an operating system and programs that make it possible for me to type out my words to convey my thoughts to you. Furthermore, someone some time ago recognized the possibility of the power of electricity, the light bulb was invented, the telephone etc. and over time many have diversified so many aspects of its use that we barely take into consideration what they have done, we simply need to charge our batteries, or have hot water and lights to see by. These inventions changed our world.

If we trace individual things back to their origin then we recognize that the world in which we live is a result of mankind's resourceful nature, our ability to invent; not create, that's God's work. Creation should be considered making something out of nothing. We as human beings can't do that but God can and has. We can take things and put them together and voila! But the "things" had to come from somewhere. How arrogant of us to think we can "create".

The point I am attempting to make is that we all depend on each other to some degree. But mostly we depend on God. Take for example the island story. When it began to rain, there was fresh water provided. You may say that this was simply nature and that how lucky you were that it rained and that you were able to capture that rain in something so you could drink the fresh water. But what about the fish and animals? How about the ability to make fire in which to cook the food? What about the oxygen in the air that you breathe? Hasn't God provided beyond our expectations or comprehension simply in the fact that we are alive? We are born, we live, we die. And during the living part we learn and grow and experience so many things. What is the purpose?

I truly hope that this book gives you the desire to have the true relationship with God I am describing. I am sure that there may be errors in some of the ways that I have related the theology to which I believe. Theology is defined as: 1) the field of study and analysis that treats of God and of God's attributes and relations to the universe; study of divine things or religious truth; divinity 2) a particular form, system, branch, or course of this study. (dictionary.com) Regardless, I hope and pray that you have looked beyond my imperfection and recognized the truth contained herein.

Now having said all of this, I encourage you to read on as I have much more to share with you. I also implore you to take on the responsibility of discovering the truth in what I present. Understand that although I may have many more years of life experience with God, I am of no more importance to Him than you. In fact, no one is; no Priest, Rabbi, Imam, Preacher, friend, acquaintance, etc. In other words, you have the right to come to God as you are. There is only one man by whom you must come to God and that man himself was God who took on the form of man. This man is Jesus. God in human form who lived a sinless life and sacrificed himself willingly so that we might have that personal relationship with God of which I have been referencing.

Now I keep injecting the name of Jesus into the mix and for many this will be controversy; and understandably so in today's world. In fact, a belief in god these days is acceptable to most people and an expectancy that everyone should respect each other's beliefs. However, the name of Jesus sets people on edge because according to his teachings, he is the only way to know God and this offends many people. I mean how dare He claim to be the only way to know God, He even claimed to BE GOD at one point. Isn't that the reason they put him to death? And the truth is that as far as man is concerned that is one of the reasons. He challenged the power system that had evolved within the Jewish religion of the day. And they could not understand how God could have a son who was also God. They had limited God. But only God should be the one doing the limiting, and He does. How else would you explain that He allowed His son to die a horrible death on a cross two thousand years ago? How else can we explain how or why He allows all the suffering and evil to exist and succeed in today's world. The only answer is that He is God and He has a plan. We aren't God and don't comprehend all of His plan because we only see what we know right now, what we are experiencing now. And that is where faith comes in the mix. We grow our faith in God's abilities and plan as we grow in our relationship to Him. So, what will you do? The choice is yours.

In the beginning was the Word, and the Word was with God, and the Word was God. John 1:1

4 Who is God?

We don't get to decide who God is, we don't get to determine who or what we think He is. We get to DISCOVER who God is as He reveals Himself to us and He does so according to the willingness and desire of our heart. God is a distinct entity. He consists of three persons in one, this is known as the Trinity. It consists of God the Father, God the Son (aka Jesus), and God the Holy Spirit. For some of you that whole idea is foreign and hard to comprehend but remember I am giving you the big picture, the details follow. The Bible tells us that God is sovereign, there is no one or no other god above Him. He is almighty, perfect and all the other big words, omniscient (all knowing) etc. He made a plan for mankind before He created the Universe and this plan was devised with mankind as its centerpiece. His plan is perfect and will ultimately be fulfilled perfectly. However, within this plan was the decision to give mankind one of the greatest gifts that He could after the gift of life itself, and that is the gift of free will, or choice. And the choices mankind made from the beginning is the reason for all of the death, pain, suffering, etc. in the world. We chose to disobey Him and follow our own path. This rebellion is also known as sin and we are all guilty of it. The Bible tells us that sin has consequences and these are the things that keep us from our relationship with Him. However, God knew that we would choose to sin and rebel against Him and He planned for the answer to the problem of sin.

God is described as many things in the Bible but the most important description of Him is not really a description but rather a definition. God is Love. He is not simply a loving God, He IS Love. And love is more of a verb than a noun. In other words, love is not love until there is some action that proves its existence. After all, you can't see love, you can't touch it, or taste it, but you can feel it. Much in the same way God Himself is. His love was made manifest in creating us. Out of the nature of who He is we were created. We are His desire, that's right God has desires but has no need for anything. So, understanding that you and I were created because He wanted us should give you pause.

"In the beginning God created the heavens and the earth." Genesis 1:1

"Then God said, Let us make mankind in our image, in our likeness, so they may rule over the fish in the sea, and birds in the sky, over the livestock and all the wild animals, and over all the creatures that move along the ground. So God created mankind in his own image, in the image of God he created them, male and female he created them. God blessed them said unto them, 'Be fruitful, and increase in number fill the earth, and subdue it. Rule over the fish in the sea, and the birds in the sky, and over every living thing that moves on the ground.'" Genesis 1:26-28

God gave us a wonderful gift in which He communicates His plan for mankind and for how to live our lives according to His divine direction. It is a book and I am sure you are familiar with it, perhaps you have even read some. This book is known to the Christian community as God's Word or the Bible. I don't know what your opinion of the Bible is, whether or not you believe it to be divinely inspired or that it's just a book of historical literature. I don't know what your opinion of Christianity and Christians is and I am trying my best to stay away from the "religious" or "self-righteous" talk with which you may have been exposed to. I understand that some of you reading this have been turned off about religion or God in general due to some bad experiences in your past. Or perhaps you actually see no real reason or benefit from embracing any religion for that matter, even Christianity. Please recall that I stated in my introduction that I believe with my whole heart that Religions are man-made but Relationship is God made. As hypocritical as this may appear, considering that Christianity is itself a religion, please contemplate this simple definition of Christianity. A Christian is a follower of Christ. Someone who places faith and trust in the teachings of Jesus of Nazareth and follows them. And this "true following" demands a relationship with Him.

God is more or less a descriptive term that we use to represent the powerful entity responsible for our existence. Many religions have names for the gods to which they give their allegiance so it is imperative that I tell you the God of which I refer to when I am describing Him and His actions. Many people believe that there is one God but there are many ways in which mankind has chosen to describe Him or understand Him. I consider this to be illogical from the standpoint that as an individual I am the same person regardless of what you call me, or how you describe me. Furthermore, I only acknowledge someone who wishes to communicate to me if they address me as I am known to myself and others who know me, by name. For example, if you call me on the phone and ask to speak to me-by name, or address a letter to me-by name, or shout my name across a crowded room to get my attention. This will tend to ensure that it is me with which you are communicating. However, you may wish to communicate to me and you may call out describing me such as "hey you, the fat bald guy in the wheelchair" or "may I speak to the man of the household" or "to the man living at such and such address". The odds are I am not acknowledging the description of me because I wish to be addressed by my name.

In the same vein I find it illogical that we tend to accept the term for God and then describe Him as "whomever you choose Him to be, or however you choose to describe Him". That's like saying to me that you can decide who I am. You may choose to see me as a fat bearded lady, or a tiger in a cage, or any number of ways and yet simply because you choose to see me or attempt to understand me in that fashion it in no way actually determines who I am. This is why we give ourselves names, why we give our children names, why we give plants and animals descriptive names and even domesticated animals such as cats and dogs names, signifying the unique aspect of who they are. It is vitally important that we understand this about THE one and TRUE God. He is unique and should be acknowledged accordingly. He should be addressed as who He is, not as who we THINK or imagine Him to be, that in itself is an arrogant and dangerous act.

There is a religion that proclaims that He, God, had a plan before He spoke the world into existence. There are many ways to describe who God is but the simplest way is to say that He is love. His creation is motivated out of love; mankind being the focus of creation. So, you can know that He created you because He loves you and wanted you. He chose to create us out of love. SO never diminish how important you are to God. Once again it is important to understand that God is not who you perceive Him to be. God doesn't adjust to our imagination of who He is. We can't simply

45

decide who we want God to be. He is a distinct person. Knowing who God is, is imperative in relating to Him. For example; you are who you are with your individual likes and dislikes, attributes that may be similar to others and yet distinctly your own. As individual as you are, God is similar in His individuality. He is distinct and unchanging which is comforting if you think about it. He doesn't change with the times nor is He undependable. He is who He says He is and you can always count on that.

It's hard to wrap our minds around an infinite God because we are finite creations. We understand beginnings and endings. Believing that God has always existed requires faith and trust. But God loves us enough to give us the ability to have this faith and trust according to our own willingness.

"So, then faith comes by hearing, and hearing by the word of God." Romans 10:17 (NKJV)

Are you willing to know God, not just your idea of who you think God is? If so then you have to utilize the tools God has supplied to begin your journey of knowing Him. The Bible is the place to begin. There is controversy in all aspects of our lives these days. Mankind's desire to be his own god and be self-determining has led to much misery and sadness. Many argue that the Bible is just a book, however the Bible proves itself over and over again to be an integrated message system from God. Some describe it as a love letter from God to man. To a non-religious person this may sound foreign and understandably so. Understanding the Bible as more than just a literary object comes with a closer relationship to God. Let me explain. The supernatural connection with God or better yet a relationship with God comes as a result of our choice.

We have the choice to determine if we want to know God or simply know about Him. The Holy Spirit being everywhere is within the believer encouraging, comforting, and growing the child of God through a personal relationship. However, the non-believer does not have the benefits of the Holy Spirit living within him and is being convicted of their need for this relationship with God.

God is sovereign meaning there is no one or no thing that is over Him. He is the final say. He is omniscient, omnipresent, omnipotent, all of these big words and one very important little word that describes Him best; LOVE. This is proven out in the fact that God is a gentleman and will not impress Himself upon someone. He loves us so much that with all His power He will not force us to choose Him, or love Him back. That is our choice. After all, would you rather have someone choose to love you or be forced to love you? So it is with God. His desire is that we choose Him back because He first chose to create us. Each one of us, individually with a unique design and plan in mind. Never discount God's ability to know you intimately, everything about you, your thoughts, actions, dreams, desires. He knows us better than we know ourselves, after all, He did plan us.

The Bible tells us that He knew us before the foundation of the world. He planned us. In fact, He planned all of creation around us but most importantly for those who would choose Him back.

"For He chose us in him before the creation of the world to be holy and blameless in his sight. In love he predestined us for adoption to sonship through Jesus Christ, in accordance with his will." Ephesians 1:4-5 (NKJV)

The book of Genesis describes the creation. He created everything before man, and for man. And it was perfect. So what happened? We screwed up is what happened. We made the choice to disobey God and go against His plan for us. This separated us and damaged our relationship because now sin had attached itself to us, and we were infected with the desire to obey our own fleshly desires rather than obey the God who made us and knows what is best for us.

When you judge according to Gods judgement, there is not one single person who does good. What we consider good before God are filthy rags. I can hear you saying; "Well, that is unbelievable! I know that I do good things, surely God recognizes the good things that I have done. I am a good person! I AM A GOOD PERSON!!!! If you are talking the Bible here then let's look at the ten commandments. I have kept most of them for all of my life! I told you before that I don't steal or lie, or cheat or kill. Why doesn't God judge me on the good things of my life because I KNOW they far outweigh the bad!!" Ok, but wait a minute, did you just say that you HAVE done some bad?

And there is our problem. Even the smallest sin is enough to separate us from God. He is Holy, Perfect, Just and must punish sin, even the smallest one. Any microbe of sin is contrary to His absolute Holiness. He cannot allow sin into His presence. Let's consider an example of a clean room here similar to where they make computer chips, or study viruses, or anywhere that from a scientific standpoint there cannot be even the most minute foreign particle that would corrupt the item that must be perfectly clean. In much the same way, in order for us to be worthy of God and His heaven even the smallest sin is the foreign particle that cannot be allowed.

God also has a government for lack of a better term. Actually, since He is God, I guess you would call it an autocracy, which is defined as a system of government by one person with absolute power. God does what He does with absolute power and with purpose. Understanding who He is, is a never-ending educational experience. After all, He is God. He is omnipotent (all powerful), omniscient (all knowing), omnipresent (everywhere), and is described as a "Trinity" understood to be made up of three distinct persons; God the Father, God the Son, and God the Holy Spirit. Let's discuss that a little more in detail. Yes, I agree that this concept of three in one is difficult to comprehend however it is possible to understand this perspective to a reasonable extent. For example, time is considered one thing and yet it has three distinct attributes; past, present, and future. Until recently the smallest known thing in the universe was an atom which is made up of three aspects: protons, neutrons, and electrons. Then science has discovered protons and neutrons are made up of three quarks each. Interesting how "three" is an aspect in many things. Water has three states of being, solid (ice), liquid, and gas (steam). Even we as human beings are considered to be made of body, soul, and spirit. I guess once again it just comes down to a question of trust or faith. I trust this defining characteristic of God because I choose to and because this trust in Him has never failed me. I also look at it logically and reason that God is God after all and who am I to question how or why. Simply because I may not fully comprehend all of God doesn't mean that it is not true. There is significantly more evidence on the scale weighing in favor of trusting His word than trusting in man's varying opinions.

To God, the most important thing is the relationship; the individual, personal relationship between you and Him. There is nothing standing in the way of this but you. Which begs the question, why don't you have one? Here's an answer; Maybe you think you do. Perhaps you have been taught, imagined or simply decided that God is who you think He is and that is how you relate to Him. God is who you THINK He is? Amazing huh?! Do you understand the arrogance in that thought process? Imagine if I decided that I know you based upon what I think you are like or who you are in reality. I decide or imagine that you are 6'2, weigh 190 pounds, have dark brown hair and brown eyes. You are a male about age 30, and you are a fisherman who also enjoys hunting. You occasionally read books and enjoy movies and your favorite food is fried chicken. Pretty good imagination huh? And I might have the odds in my favor that someone who fits that description may someday read this and be amazed!

But the truth is that just because I imagined that you are who I described doesn't mean that is who you are. Let's say that I am a fan of a famous actor or athlete so I read everything I can about them, watch all of their movies, watch videos of previous games in which they have performed. I study about them till I am exhausted and think I know them very well indeed. It still doesn't mean that I know them personally. I would have to meet them someway, face to face, Facetime, Zoom, text, however and have some kind of personal interaction with them to truly get a glimpse of who this person is. They in turn would have to agree to the relationship, they would have to agree to reveal aspects of who they are and I would do likewise. And let's say that we find a common bond and I get to know them by spending time with them and their friends and family. They tell me stories about their knowledge and relationship to this person. This builds our relationship and as time progresses, I have a meaningful relationship with them based upon personal experience not just information that I have acquired. This is the same way it is with God. You can read and be taught, go to religious gatherings, church, concerts, etc. and NEVER have a personal relationship with God. Because it is all up to you. You have to make the choice to know God. Remember, He knows you already better than you know yourself because He created you. He knew exactly when you would be alive, your likes and dislikes, your talents, your potential. He sees and knows you so very well and desires for you to know Him back so that you can work together in this magnificent adventure called life.

Perhaps you think that you can simply put a bunch of religious ideas about God together and make Him an amalgamation of the attributes that you want in a "God". Perhaps you enjoy nature and so you decide that you will worship your idea of God through nature. After all, you are a good person, you have a high morality, you don't steal or tell lies. You have a good work ethic and are a good employee, you take care of your family and treat them well. You treat others well also; you even give to charitable organizations that do-good works and help those less fortunate than yourself. And you have decided that if there is a God and an afterlife, then you should have nothing to fear because you have led a good life and consider yourself to be a good person. Well, that sounds all good and well and even Hollywood would agree with you as over the years they have produced many movies with just that sort of morality. Good wins in the end and evil is punished. The "good" people go to heaven and the "bad" people go to hell. Sounds logical and somewhat reasonable right? It feels right, I hope that I have been good enough, I have faith in myself that I am a good person. If there is a God and morality is something that He created for us to live by then on the scales of whether or not I am a good person deserving heaven then I would say that I have a really good chance. However, there is a problem with that way of thinking. The Bible states it very plainly and several times:

"The fool has said in his heart that there is no God. They are corrupt, they have done abominable works, THERE IS NONE WHO DOES GOOD." Psalm 14:1

"They have all turned aside, they have together become corrupt; THERE IS NONE WHO DOES GOOD, NO, NOT ONE." Psalm 14:3

"The fool has said in his heart, there is no God, they are corrupt and have done abominable iniquity; THERE IS NONE WHO DOES GOOD." PSALM 53:1

"Every one of them has turned aside; they have together become corrupt; THERE IS NONE WHO DOES GOOD, NO, NOT ONE." Psalm 53:3

"They have all turned aside; they have together become unprofitable; THERE IS NONE WHO DOES GOOD, NO, NOT ONE." Romans 3:12 (NKJV)

Getting the picture yet? How about this;

"But we are all like an unclean thing. AND ALL OUR RIGHTEOUSNESSES ARE LIKE FILTHY RAGS; We all fade as a leaf, and our iniquities, like the wind, have taken us away." Isaiah 64:6 (NKJV)

Let's remember that God has no need for anything. He is perfect. He is self-sufficient. He is also is all of those big words, Omniscient meaning all knowing, Omnipresent meaning everywhere, Omnipotent meaning all powerful, so there is no guess work for God. He doesn't have to do something and hope for an outcome. He already knows the outcome. And He has taken into account every variable. And I know what you are thinking, then why did He create a world that is imperfect, so full of hatred, sadness, evil, pain, etc. We have discussed this but let's just re-emphasize it. When God determined that He would create mankind, and make no mistake, creation is all about mankind, He knew He would have to give us choice. Well, He didn't have to, He chose to. You see He could have created us as obedient beings. Perfect without evil being a part of our existence; but that's not God. Whenever I am discussing this topic with someone, I always ask this question. "Would you rather have someone choose to love you, or be forced to love you?" And the answer is always the same. Everyone wants someone to choose to love them. And so it is with God. He did not want puppets on strings or mind numbed robots. So, we had to have choice, and there is no choice if evil doesn't exist; the choice between good and evil. Now wait just a minute, are you saying that God created evil? No, I am saying that God created the opportunity for evil to exist. God is good. The opposite of good is not nothing. It is evil.

As I have stated before, we were created for love. To know love, experience love, give and receive love. The Bible tells us that God is love. Therefore, we were created to know God. He knows us. He has always known us. Let that sink in. God is eternal; no beginning, no ending. He has always been and will always be. And as a part of being God He knows everything and He makes no mistakes. Therefore, you are not a mistake, rather a planned creation that He loves with a love that is hard to comprehend. He designed you, and placed you in his creation at exactly the right time in which He wanted you to be. This was done out of love because God is love and He loves like no one else ever has or ever will. He loves you so much that he gave you a will of your own to determine how you will respond to him. He created you out of His desire. The God who created the universe and everything in it wanted you. No, in fact he loves you so much that he gave you one of the greatest gifts that He could bestow, and that gift is choice. He wants you to choose to love him back. He wants you to choose to collaborate with him regarding your life. He has a perfect plan for your life but we all know that we don't live in a perfect world. However, he has the capability, power, and desire to adjust his plan according to your actions. Depending upon your willingness to collaborate with him regarding your life the consequences may be beneficial or detrimental. It's your choice. What do you believe?

You may say that you never had that choice but I beg to differ. You have that choice now. In fact, the reason you are reading this right now is no mistake, and don't you believe it is. However your eyes landed upon this page know that The God of the Universe is reaching out to you again, to tell you He wants you to know Him, personally. Now that may sound arrogant but it is not. It's not me who created all there is. I am not God, way too big a job for me. What I am is a man with a heart that has known Him for some time with a whole bunch of evidence that proves I know what I am saying. The most important part is that I have witnessed God's power to turn something bad into good. Let me explain; probably like you, I have experienced some of the most horrible events in my life. Perhaps you have experienced much worse and this is common to all people because we live in a world that is separated from God because of our rejection of Him and His ways. Let's call it what it is and what God's word calls it, SIN. Yeah, I am trying not to sound "churchy: or "preachy" but the truth is that you hear most of what I am telling you in churches, by a preacher. And thank God for them because there would not be the number of children of God there are without these two. But let's get one thing straight. Religion is man-made, RELATIONSHIP is God made. This relationship is only possible one way and that is through the person of Jesus. In fact, the only way to become a child of God, to be adopted into His family is through being born again.

" But as many as received Him, to them He gave the right to become the children of God, to those who believe in His Name." John 1:12 (NKJV)

Let's talk about that.

And the Word became flesh and dwelt among us, and we beheld His glory, the glory as of the only begotten of the Father, full of grace and truth. John 1:14

5 Who Is Jesus?

There was a Jewish man named Jesus who lived in a village called Nazareth approximately 2000 years ago. This village was in the country known today as Israel. We know about him and his life because of the ministry of his life that was written down by eyewitnesses to his teachings, miracles, death, burial, resurrection, and ascent into Heaven. These writings were compiled with others that were also composed during a period of approximately 50 years following his ascent; This according to various historical scholars. They are what is known as today as the New Testament of the Holy Bible. They are accepted as a true witness to the life of Jesus, his ministry, and the early church that began as a result. The acceptance is not only from a religious perspective but also from a historical perspective. This is due to the number of actual copies of original manuscripts and the fact that they are dated so close to the actual events of his life. For example, the book of Mark which is known as one of the four Gospels is believed to have been written approximately 30 years after Jesus' death, burial, and resurrection and this would have been a time in which others who were alive to bear witness to these accounts could have easily refuted them. And there are approximately 24,000 copies of the New Testament copied in various languages in comparison to 9 of "The Jewish War" by first century historian Josephus, 30 of Plato's writings, and 650 of

Homer's Iliad. This is logical justification to the fact of the life of this man Jesus and his ministry.

I tell you these things so that you will understand that there should be no doubt as to whether or not this Jesus of Nazareth was a real human being that lived approximately 2000 years ago. What he did with his life and ministry and what you believe about that fact is the sole basis for this book. Jesus of Nazareth claimed to be God in the flesh, come to earth to suffer and die for the sins of mankind; The sins that have kept the world from a relationship with God the Father. He also claimed that he and the Father were one and the same. Furthermore, he taught that after he ascended into Heaven, he would send the Holy Spirit who could actually regenerate the dead spirit of man caused by sin, and indwell man as a result of being Born Again. Let's look at what the Bible tells us from this interaction between Jesus and a member of the religious community of the time known as Nicodemus.

The Gospel of John Chapter 3:1-21 (NKJV)

There was a man of the Pharisees named Nicodemus, a ruler of the Jews. This man came to Jesus by night and said to Him, "Rabbi, we know that You are a teacher come from God; for no one can do these signs that You do unless God is with him."

Jesus answered and said to him, "Most assuredly, I say to you, unless one is born again, he cannot see the kingdom of God."

Nicodemus said to Him, "How can a man be born when he is old? Can he enter a second time into his mother's womb and be born?"

Jesus answered, "Most assuredly, I say to you, unless one is born of water and the Spirit, he cannot enter the kingdom of God. That which is born of the flesh is flesh, and that which is born of the Spirit is spirit. Do not marvel that I said to you, 'You must be born again.' The wind blows where it wishes, and you hear the sound of it, but cannot tell where it comes from and where it goes. So is everyone who is born of the Spirit."

Nicodemus answered and said to Him, "How can these things be?"

Jesus answered and said to him, "Are you the teacher of Israel, and do not know these things? Most assuredly, I say to you, We speak what We know and testify what We have seen, and you do not receive Our witness. If I have told you earthly things and you do not believe, how will you believe if I tell you heavenly things? No one has ascended to heaven but He who came down from heaven, that is, the Son of Man who is in heaven. And as Moses lifted up the serpent in the wilderness, even so must the Son of Man be lifted up, that whoever believes in Him should not perish but have eternal life. For God so loved the world that He gave His only begotten Son, that whoever believes in Him should not perish but have everlasting life. For God did not send His Son into the world to condemn the world, but that the world through Him might be saved.

"He who believes in Him is not condemned; but he who does not believe is condemned already, because he has not believed in the name of the only begotten Son of God. And this is the condemnation, that the light has come into the world, and men loved darkness rather than light, because their deeds were evil. For everyone practicing evil hates the light and does not come to the light, lest his deeds should be exposed. But he who does the truth comes to the light, that his deeds may be clearly seen, that they have been done in God."

So, Jesus tells us through this scripture of his purpose on earth in the lives of mankind. We have always been in need of a Savior since Adam and Eve sinned in the Garden of Eden. That sin has been passed onto all of us from that time and although we were not in the Garden ourselves to make that choice then, sadly we do so today and have our whole lives because it is the nature of who we are. We are fallen and separated from God, a God who knew before the foundation of the earth that we would need a Savior, and so He Himself became that Savior. But from what do we need saving? God is Holy and Just and according to His Righteous Judgement He must punish sin. So, there is a price to be paid for our sins.

"For the wages of sin is death, but the gift of God is eternal life in Christ Jesus our Lord." Romans 6:23 (NKJV)

So according to God's law death is the payment for our sins. And this death continues our separation from a loving God who never wanted us to die in the first place. No, He created mankind (Adam and Eve) perfect, sinless and yet He knew that without choice His love could not be made fully manifested in our relationship to Him. Love is more of an action than a feeling. It is also something that you cannot see but can be felt. So, He allowed for the opportunity for evil to exist so that we would have the choice. And that choice is to whether or not we will accept or reject Him.

There is one more important truth for you to know before you dig deeper into what I have written here and although it may be confusing nonetheless it is the truth; not my truth but God's truth. When Jesus came to earth to offer himself as salvation for us, he also wanted us to know more about God. Until he came and taught us so much about God the Father, and that he was God's son, mankind had always understood God to be one, and only one. The concept that Jesus could be God also is what the Jews considered blasphemy worthy of death but through his resurrection he proved that He was God also, that He actually is God's Son. He further taught that there was a third person of the God Head, God the Holy Spirit. So, a major aspect of Jesus' teaching was that God was in fact one God made of three distinct persons; God the Father, God the Son, and God the Holy Spirit.

"In the beginning God created the heavens and the earth." Genesis 1:1(NKJV)

"Then God said, Let US make mankind in OUR image, in OUR likeness, so they may rule over the fish in the sea, and birds in the sky, over the livestock and all the wild animals, and over all the creatures that move along the ground. So, God created mankind in his own image, in the image of God he created them, male and female he created them. God blessed them said unto them, 'Be fruitful, and increase in number fill the earth, and subdue it. Rule over the fish in the sea, and the birds in the sky, and over every living thing that moves on the ground.'" Genesis 1:26-28

This concept may be hard to comprehend and yet it is true. This is known as the Trinity, not three God's in one, but One God in three persons. I go into greater detail later but I will give you some points to ponder.

First, I repeat again that we don't get to decide who or what God is, we get to discover who He is if we are willing to believe what He reveals to us. He has given us many evidences that this three in one aspect is not unusual in His creation. For example, water, which covers most of the earth and is approximately 50% of the substance of which our own physical bodies consist, can be three different attributes: ice which is solid, steam which is gas, and liquid. Three attributes of one thing. Also, time consists of past, present, and future and yet is considered one thing.

Jesus told His disciples before He ascended into Heaven that it was good that He was going back to be with the Father so that He would send the "Helper".

"Nevertheless, I tell you the truth. It is to your advantage that I go away; for if I do not go away, the Helper will not come to you; but if I depart, I will send Him to you. And when He has come, He will convict the world of sin, and of righteousness, and of judgment: of sin, because they do not believe in Me; of righteousness, because I go to My Father and you see Me no more; of judgment, because the ruler of this world is judged.

"I still have many things to say to you, but you cannot bear them now. However, when He, the Spirit of truth, has come, He will guide you into all truth; for He will not speak on His own authority, but whatever He hears He will speak; and He will tell you things to come. He will glorify Me, for He will take of what is Mine and declare it to you. All things that the Father has are Mine. Therefore, I said that He will take of Mine and declare it to you." John 16:7-15 (NKJV)

Furthermore, He instructed His disciples;

"Go therefore and make disciples of all the nations, baptizing them in the name of the Father and of the Son and of the Holy Spirit, teaching them to observe all things that I have commanded you; and lo, I am with you always, even to the end of the age." Matthew 28:19-20 (NKJV)

The Holy Spirit is the aspect of God that is omnipresent meaning everywhere. God the Father is in Heaven and seated at His right hand is Jesus. The Holy Spirit also described as the "Helper," or "Comforter" is the Spirit of God that gives us rebirth spiritually when we are "Born Again". This is what Jesus was talking about when He was telling Nicodemus that you must be born again in order to see the Kingdom of Heaven. It is in fact a supernatural occurrence that happens when you choose to make Jesus the Lord of your life and this happens when we first recognize our sinfulness and how it has prevented us from a relationship with God. God wants us to choose Him and His ways and this requires that we repent or turn away from our sins and choose His plan and direction for our lives. And when we are Born Again our spiritual connection with God is renewed and we become His children by adoption into the family of God. This is all as a result of believing that Jesus is who He claimed to be, the Son of God.

"If you confess with your mouth the Lord Jesus and believe in your heart that God has raised Him from the dead, you will be saved. For with the heart one believes unto righteousness, and with the mouth confession is made unto salvation." Romans 10:9-10 (NKJV)

"But as many as received Him, to them He gave the right to become children of God, to those who believe in His name: who were born, not of blood, nor of the will of the flesh, nor of the will of man, but of God." John 1:12-13 (NKJV)

Other religions offer an afterlife but they require your work in order for you to achieve this gift. And Jesus Himself stated that He is the only way to God the Father and an eternity in Heaven with Him.

"Jesus said to him, 'I am the way, the truth, and the life. No one comes to the Father except through Me.'" John 14:6 (NJKV)

As I stated earlier, I don't believe in coincidences. It is not a coincidence that you are reading this. The one and only Living, all powerful, creator of the Universe is reaching out to you to reveal Himself to you so that you may make the choice to choose Him or reject Him. You don't have to believe me, right now wherever you are you have the right to ask Him to reveal to you whether or not what I present to you here is true or not. I know God's power and love are limitless and He knows what is in your heart, if the desire to know Him is there or not. I am going to teach you how God created you and me out of love. How He knew He would have to give us choice because He did not want puppets or robots, rather people who would choose to love Him back. And most importantly He wants us to choose Him back out of love, not fear. Yes, the truth is that we are separated from Him because of sin and He is a Holy and Just God and will punish sin. However, He made a way for us not to be the ones punished for this sin through the person of His only begotten Son, Jesus. And what that requires is faith and a decision to reject sin and request His forgiveness.

The Bible tells us that God is sovereign, there is no one or no other god above Him. He is almighty, perfect and all the other big words, omniscient (all knowing) etc. He made a plan for mankind before He created the Universe and this plan was devised with mankind as its centerpiece. His plan is perfect and will ultimately be fulfilled perfectly. However, within this plan was the decision to give mankind one of the greatest gifts that He could after the gift of life itself, and that is the gift of free will, or choice. And the choices mankind made from the beginning is the reason for all of the death, pain, suffering, etc. in the world. We chose to disobey Him and follow our own path. This rebellion is also known as sin and we are all guilty of it. The Bible tells us that sin has consequences and these are the things that keep us from our relationship with Him. However, God knew that we would choose to sin and rebel against Him and He planned for the answer to the problem of sin.

God is described as many things in the Bible but the most important description of Him is not really a description but rather a definition. God is Love. He is not simply a loving God, He IS Love. And love is more of a verb than a noun. In other words, love is not love until there is some action that proves its existence. After all, you can't see love, you can't touch it, or taste it, but you can feel it. Much in the same way God Himself is. His love was made manifest in creating us. Out of the nature of who He is we were created. We are His desire, that's right God has desires but has no need for anything. So, understanding that you and I were created because He wanted us should give you pause. The proof that God wanted us is in our DNA. One of the most important scientific discoveries in the past few decades has been the human genome. DNA proves that each one of us is a unique individual that will never be duplicated. How can you get more specific than that? As human beings we share roughly 99% of the same genes and yet that 1% difference is what makes you exclusive. Your particular hair color, eyes, the shape of your nose, your body height, freckles, moles, singing ability, sports capability, your intelligence, where you were born, grew up, who your parents are, who your friends are, all these things make you who YOU are, and God wanted YOU. Every person God created has a unique DNA that sets us apart from each other. Furthermore, God proved that He is love by becoming a man himself;

"And the Word became flesh and dwelt among us, and we beheld His glory, the glory as of the only begotten of the Father, full of grace and truth." John 1:14 (NKJV)

Jesus also lived a sinless life to fulfill the righteousness required by God's law, and died a horrible death on the cross to pay the price for our sin so that we could be reconciled to God.

"But God demonstrates His own love toward us, in that while we were still sinners, Christ died for us." Romans 5:8 (NKJV)

If any of you lacks wisdom let him ask of God who giveth to all men liberally and without reproach, and it will be given to him.

James 1:5

6 Wisdom

Wisdom
noun: the quality of having experience, knowledge, and good judgment; the quality of being wise. (Apple Dictionary)

There is a big difference between intelligence and wisdom. Someone can be really smart but not very wise. I consider wisdom to be knowing what to do with your intelligence or "smarts." Consequently, I really am confounded by people who don't believe in God. I certainly am arrogant about a lot of things concerning my life but even I understand that there has to be something responsible for all of this. The Universe is too huge and amazingly complex for it just to have happened. And it seems like science every day comes up with some new amazing discovery or advancement for mankind. The absolutely amazing discovery and defining of DNA in the human genome has to give any reasonable person pause when trying to legitimize evolution. I mean come on, the intricate detail and apparent design of a human cell? Each cell is a little machine that has the ability to replicate, repair, and function in its capacity that it is designed to achieve. And there are literally trillions of cells in our bodies! And we are supposed to believe that this happened by accident? I don't have the faith for that theory but I do know that there is a God who designed this Universe and this world in which we live, and more importantly each one of us. Therefore, I don't understand people who believe in God but just act as if He isn't important. It seems logical to me that any reasonable person who believes in God must expect that He is concerned with detail and design. And if that is true then how can He not be interested in us human beings considering that we are the most amazing creature on the planet?

Then doesn't it stand to reason that God wants us to know Him? Doesn't that make the most sense when you try to understand the reason for your existence? There must be a purpose in your being here alive on this planet right now, and if so, what is it? Maybe you feel like this: I don't know what to believe. I don't know if I even believe anything. I feel like I am just existing and there really is no purpose in my life. After all, if evolution is true then what is the purpose of life because it has no lasting meaning? If this is all that there is then what's the point? I mean really, I've been taught my whole life that we are evolved from apes that come from a single celled organism that just "happened" to appear, and that everything in our universe just" began" billions of years ago. But I am expected to believe this and not to challenge it and just to go along like most of my friends. Occasionally we find a project that is worth our time; political, charitable, you know the kind of stuff to get your blood pressure up and you feel like you are accomplishing something of value. But what can you possibly be accomplishing that has value when in 100 years it's all forgotten or meaningless to the people who are alive then? Does this sound familiar?

What do you want out of life? Happiness? Success? Wealth? Fame? Purpose? Some would say that most of these are connected to some degree and that they are relative to each individual's station in life such as where you were born, your upbringing, your family's business etc. For example, if your family were farmers it is more than likely you may choose farming. If your parents were doctors, lawyers, or business people, you may choose to follow along those lines. The contributing factor in this is happiness. Most children seek to follow in their parents' footsteps because they consider the happiness that they have experienced growing up to be a positive blueprint for their lives. However, everyone doesn't have a happy childhood so the opposite may be true. The choice to reject the family influence and strike out in new direction is what makes us individuals.

OK, so you have children and want a better life for them than you had, it's a common desire. Why? What does it matter if we are all here by accident? If we are just some cosmic joke what is the purpose of trying to make a difference? If there are aliens from other planets, where did they come from? Why haven't they contacted us? And if they are evolved creatures also, then what is the point of their life? If we are just here by accident, evolved creatures of the short lifespan, then isn't our existence in essence hopeless?

Death; now here is the subject that answers seem to evade everyone from everywhere. Death offends me. I don't like it and I never have from an early age. Maybe it's because my father died when I was 6 years old. Death is such a weird subject to begin with. So, we die but our Ghost lives on? Or our "spirit" lives on, and how does this jibe with evolution. What is the purpose of a spirit? If you believe in evolution, then why is there death? Seems to me that we should have evolved to where death is not necessary. Absurd you say? Everything dies! But why? Hmmmm. Reincarnation, Paradise, Heaven, Nirvana… we don't seem to like the death issue so we have decided that there must be something AFTER death, something worth living life for.

Perhaps I am being a little too blunt here. But what is wrong with blunt? What is wrong with matter-of-fact? Wouldn't you rather have someone tell you something that's absolutely true rather than beat around the bush and you wonder forever? The trouble with that today is this expressing absolute truth is not so readily acceptable. Everyone wants to be offended by something. I am not sure how this began but it's gotten out of hand and it's ridiculous, nevertheless this is what we have to deal with.

I have answers. They are answers to questions you have, that you want, and that you need. I am not saying this arrogantly, I am saying this with confidence knowing that if I were in your shoes, I would want someone to tell me the absolute truth also. Yeah, you probably heard similar things before. Messages from people trying to sell you something, wanting to get your hopes up about something, someone or someplace you place your faith in then disappointed you. Well, the difference here is that I will give you the information and what you do with it, the resulting consequences, are your responsibility. You see I am not here to sell you something. Well, that's not really true, I have sold you this book, but that's where it ends for me. You may have heard it said that you can't want something for someone more than they want it for themselves, so I am hoping and praying that you really want answers. There are absolutes, do you believe that?

This is the history of mankind; Continual choice. Where do we go from here? We all want answers. We want to know. We live in a day and age of instant information. Some of it is correct and some not. But we want to be right in our knowledge. We want to have the right information so that we can make decisions based upon what is right, what is true. The logical reasoning being that decisions have consequences and these choices we make affect our lives and those whom we love. We all want similar results, health, happiness, and success to name some of the most prevalent ones.

Our cultures dictate our choices whether we like it or not. The initial influences in our lives mold and shape us into the thinking that direct these decisions and if we are wise, we must be willing to question our cultures. We question to determine if the traditions or philosophy of our ways of life are worthwhile, in fact true, or simply a continuation of customary lifestyles. If we are blessed these classic traditions serve us well and we can continue these choices. If we are ill-at-ease with them, we may choose to change and improve them. The wisdom is in knowing what to do.

One of the time-honored traditions throughout human history is religion. Belief systems that comprise mankind's desire to recognize, honor and worship a being greater than himself. The recognition that life comes from somewhere or something outside of ourselves and the need to acknowledge this is considered faith. Throughout the course of human history these faiths have formed cultures, influenced multitudes, and even established nations. These religions, organized by man with dictates, tenets, and requirements, have led those outside of these belief systems to question why a being worth worshiping would have so many demands. Therefore, it is reasonable to suggest that religion is manmade whereas relationship is God made. As far as God is concerned, a relationship is the objective not the confines of an organized set of rules and regulations established by man.

However, we must not discount the fact that a God who created this universe as well as mankind does in fact have rules or laws that He has established. And we should recognize that God being a supreme, all knowing being must have ordained these laws with a perfect purpose. Furthermore, we should consider that many of these man-made religions initially sought to determine these laws outside of God's influence thereby corrupting God's desire for relationship. So, it stands to reason why so many reject organized religion with the concession that religion is not the answer and therefore God will judge us according to our behavior. And if in fact God judges us and there is more than just this life in which we live, then He will take into consideration our intentions instead of our actions. But this flies in the face of God having laws that He established with a perfect purpose.

Somewhat confusing to say the least. Understandable why so many people simply live their lives without giving credit to the God to whom credit is due. If you acknowledge God then you have to attempt to understand Him, and to many this endeavor seems quite futile. But it doesn't have to be.

The greatest gift bestowed upon mankind, second only to life itself, has been the gift of freedom. The freedom to choose. If God had simply wanted robots or puppets on strings who would obey His every desire without question, He most assuredly could have created them. But why would He do this? Even we, as imperfect human beings, understand the fundamental desire for others to choose to love us rather than being forced to do so. Therefore, doesn't it stand to reason that God would do the same? If God is a loving God, why should He not desire likewise? I believe that He does and thus the reason for creating mankind with the freedom to choose to love Him back. We were created to love, be loved, experience love which is the ultimate goal of bringing glory to God. When asked many religious people will tell you that they believe that we were created to bring glory to God without truly understanding the many aspects of what that means. In my opinion, bringing glory to God is becoming more like Him as in the reflection given by looking in a mirror. And becoming more like Him is only possible by having a relationship with Him made possible through belief in Jesus.

Ok so where does this leave us? If religion is not God's idea and relationship is, then how do we achieve this act of choosing to love Him back without some kind of organized way of doing so? Well, first of all let's understand the term "religion." The dictionary defines religion in this way: 1) the belief in and worship of a superhuman controlling power, especially a personal God or gods, 2) a particular system of faith and worship 3) a pursuit or interest to which someone ascribes supreme importance.(dictionary.com)

So, religion, by these definitions, place us in the position of determining the form in which we choose to define God. The term "personal God or gods" is interesting in that it allows for our interpretation of who God is. Does this seem reasonable? Do others get to determine who you are by their opinion, estimation, or perspective of you; Or are you in fact simply who you are? If someone wants to truly know you, they must invest time with you, learn who you are and have a relationship with you. And so it is with God. The mistake so many make in their pursuit of God is their attempt to make Him into who they want Him to be rather than discover who He is.

If we believe in God then it is our choice as to what degree we want to know Him. If we recognize that He is an all-powerful, all knowing being then we must recognize that if He chose to create us then it stands to reason that He must have some purpose in doing so. Furthermore, doesn't it also make sense that He desires for us to know Him, not just about Him? It is rational to believe that He yearns for us to want to know Him, for us to learn who He is and His purpose for our being.

We have the tendency to deny God this "human" quality. In fact, there are religions that describe God as being beyond our comprehension, too magnificent for our human minds to understand. This belief diminishes God by limiting His abilities. Doesn't it make sense that God has the ability to meet us at any level of our comprehension? Has He not created us knowing every intimate detail of our being including what we are and are not able to comprehend? And if He created us, He no doubt did it with purpose and because He is all knowing doesn't it stand to reason that He realizes the challenges we will face in our endeavor to know Him?

We all want to be right. We want to know that what we believe is right. We all have a world view that has been shaped by our life experiences such as where we grew up, and what type of socioeconomic environment to which we were exposed. Hopefully as we mature, we are willing to accept that perhaps some of the things we once believed are not completely right. We learn to adjust our way of thinking, subsequently adjusting how we in fact behave. As we age, we discover that there are certain things that remain constant, take for example gravity. I have fallen at 3 years old and I have fallen at 59 years old and although it may hurt a bit more at 59, the constant factor has been gravity. The sun also appears every day, although at times I may not see it for the clouds are blocking my view, but I have the faith that it is still there providing what this planet and its inhabitants need to sustain life. And much like the feeling of pain from falling I feel the sun's effects on my body and my eyes can see because of the light it provides. So, we understand absolutes do exist, meaning that there are things that are unchangeable regardless of our opinion or belief. For some this is very difficult to admit and for others it is understandably a fact of life. And although life is constantly changing, we can rest assured that there are some things that will remain the same. To me that is very comforting. I have learned that boundaries and limitations are a very important aspect to understanding. Boundaries with myself and others, my relationships to them and my own limitations physically and emotionally have given me a sense of peace that I recognize as an uncommon trend these days.

What is important to recognize in all of this is that God is real and awesome and somewhat beyond our comprehension, however, He took all of this into consideration when He designed us. The Bible tells us that we are created in His image, His likeness.

Many times, we make the arrogant mistake of making God in our image, our likeness. It is valuable to us to understand that God is magnificent and so much of who He is we cannot comprehend but there is so much that He wants us to comprehend. He wants us to know Him. To have an intimate relationship with Him; each one of us, individually. We diminish God if we believe that He does not have the power to do this. We say that there are billions of people on earth, how could he want to have a relationship with me? I suggest to you that God is so powerful and awesome that He certainly has the capability to know each of us individually and intimately. In fact, it is His desire to do so. Yes, God has desires. The Bible tells us this.

"It is not His desire that any should perish, but that all should come to repentance." 2 Peter 3:9 (NKJV)

He has no need for He is self-sufficient and can have and do anything within His nature. His nature is such that there are things He cannot and will not do. For example, He cannot learn. He already knows everything. More importantly for us to remember is that we cannot disappoint Him because He already knows what we are going to do.

Let's get back to what I stated earlier, that we were created to love, be loved, experience love etc. God being the ultimate example of love being what we should desire and aspire to be like. Not an aspiration to be God, but to be like Him in love. And isn't it interesting that love is not a tangible thing? You can't touch love, see love or taste love. There are so many things that we ascribe to love. I love pizza. I love my wife. I love that way my daughters laugh. However, I can't point to love and have you go and get some for me. Love to many is an action. I believe for God it most definitely is.

The fact that you were created is an important issue for you to decide to be true. The lie of evolution is one that is designed by an enemy, to deceive us into discounting Him. Without God we are simply a cosmic accident. We just happened; and in truth that really makes no sense. The universe, the earth and all that is within it, especially us and our design screams that there was and is a creator. He has always been and therefore He is the cause of everything that there is; that's it plain pure and simple.

Now faith is the substance of things hoped for, the evidence of things not seen. Hebrews 11:1

7 Faith

Faith
    noun: a complete trust or confidence in someone or something (Apple Dictionary)

What is faith? Faith is belief in something, confidence or trust in something. We all have it, to one degree or another. We all begin our lives with faith. When we are very young, even as helpless babies we have faith. Even though at the time we don't understand it we are exercising faith by crying out in need. As a result, someone comes to meet our needs. When we are hungry, we get fed, when we need changing, we get our diapers changed. So, we learn to have the faith that our needs are going to be met. It may not sound like the faith that you may be thinking of as in religion but at its core, this is faith. Follow this even further, the baby has faith that their needs will be met because even in their short span of life their little brains are reasoning. Their brains are working: "I need something because something is uncomfortable"; the "I am hungry"-cry. You may be thinking that this is simply a natural action, something that just happens. But don't forget that the brain has to send a signal for the physical act of crying. There is a scientific reason for actions caused by the brain. And this begins inside the mother's womb. Babies feel, and they sleep, move, kick, etc. Just ask any mother if it is not true that their baby began its personality inside of their womb. There is reason involved. The brain is reasoning that this need has to be met because the situation has to change, after all, it has before; logic. And as the baby is crying, they are hoping that because of their action of crying, something will happen. "will I be fed? Will someone change me? Will someone please pick me up?" …emotion. Of course, the crying is emotion, a feeling of sadness or anger or frustration because of a need. And when these needs are met, a natural, or better yet, God given event occurs; love. The beginnings of our understanding of love begin the moment we are conceived. We can know this because we are created by God in His image, in His likeness; and God IS love.

I know, that sounds like a roundabout way to make a point but I still think it's a great point! We all exhibit faith in our lives whether we are aware of it or not. And that faith is a result of some choice we made. For instance, you are reading what I have written right now. You made a choice, you have some modicum of faith that you aren't wasting your time and that hopefully what you read will either be entertaining, enlightening or both. I hope to provide both, please continue to have faith. The faith thing is important to recognize and understand. There are so many rather simple things that we do, without thinking that require our faith. If we are sitting down in a chair, we have exercised faith that it will hold us up. We just saw someone get up from it so our faith in it is justified. We do this without really thinking about it because we have done it literally hundreds of times and hopefully without a bad consequence like it breaking out from underneath us. And I know this because I have had one break beneath me! However, I still sit in chairs, I just pay a little closer attention to their sturdiness.

We also place our faith in others. The people at the electric company, the waterworks, etc., people we don't often think of unless you work in one of these industries. Yet out of sheer habit and expectance we turn on the light switch and have faith that the lights will work. Or we turn on the water spigot and are confident that if we have paid the bill, water will flow. And if we have fuel in our automobile, we have faith that it will start and take us where we need to go. So, we exercise faith in so many ways each and every day. So why is it that we tend to doubt our ability to exercise faith when it comes to God?

We can say we have faith in something but we must act on that faith for it to be meaningful. Reasonably acknowledging or simply observing the actions of others adds justification to your faith, but for it to be meaningful you must act on it. And so, you begin to exercise your faith but in order to do so you have to believe something will happen. Your team will win. It won't rain this Saturday. You have to believe in yourself. No matter how small that hope is, it requires faith. Maybe the faith is based upon past experiences. Your team has had a great season thus far. It's the dry season so it shouldn't rain. You have been doing so well on the goals you have set for yourself…Faith. So much of our daily existence requires a great deal of faith whether or not we are willing to admit it. You may not even recognize that you exercise your faith consistently without even realizing it or acknowledging it.

The Bible tells us that without faith it is impossible to please God.

"But without faith it is impossible to please Him, for He who comes to God must believe that He is, and that He is a rewarder of those who diligently seek Him." Hebrews 11:6 (NKJV)

Actually, I will go further and say that without faith it is impossible to know God. First you must believe that there is a God. That in itself requires faith. Many people believe in God. They believe that there is something somewhere holding everything together. They may even know others who believe in God. And these people believe in God in different ways. There are so many different religions in this world. SO many in fact that it can become confusing as to which one should you place your faith. This is why I have stated from the beginning that religion is man-made and relationship is God made. God did not author all of these religions. He is not the God of confusion. He desires for us to know Him so why would He make the path unclear? The answer is that He did not. There is an enemy at work that desires to keep you from this relationship with God in any and all ways possible. This enemy hates God with the greatest passion and hates God's creation with even more. This enemy is called Satan, the adversary and was once one of God's top angels. The Bible tells us that He was the most beautiful and glorious. Then pride overtook him and he desired to BE GOD. He wanted what God had, and continues to want it today. And since he cannot have it, he will do whatever he can to destroy it for everyone and everything else. Do you know anyone like this? Someone who wants to be king of the hill all the time. Someone who wants to be the lord of the manor, and throws a fit when they don't get their way? Well, in truth we all have this attribute. It is a result of sin. Our desire to dictate our existence in whatever way we deem acceptable. We don't want to answer to anyone. We want to make the rules and want everyone else to abide by them. The problem is that if everyone makes their own rules eventually, they will not agree with each other and problems will arise. Just look at history for that lesson.

Faith is a small word in the number of actual letters; however, it has a big meaning. Some people associate the word faith with religious beliefs. "my faith teaches me this" or "I am of the such and such religious faith…" but the action of faith is more comprehensible. For example; you may have seen an airplane flying. You may even know people who have flown before and you are sure that if you chose to fly somewhere you would make it. But you have to actually get on the airplane to exercise that faith. Think on that for a moment; You can believe or "have faith" that an airplane will fly because you have seen them take off, fly, land, etc. You may have even picked up people from the airport after a flight. You probably know many people who have flown. And yet you may never have actually gotten on an airplane and travelled anywhere. You have yet to act on your faith. Acting on your faith requires that YOU get into the airplane and fly in it. You can believe something all day, but until you ACT on your belief, the faith is not real, or it is in effect, dead.

I am going to ask you to have faith in yourself. I want you to believe enough in yourself that you understand that you have been given one of the greatest gifts in life and that is the gift of choice. The ability to choose. Perhaps I should qualify that and say rationally choose. What separates us from the animals is the ability to rationally choose. Animals choose all the time mostly by instinct or habit. We on the other hand have the brain power to study and learn and use this knowledge to choose. So, I want you to use that ability to understand that you have a choice. You get to choose to believe what I say here or not to believe it; to agree or disagree. But the choice is yours, and yours alone. Do you have faith?

One of the most profound questions we ask in our lives is "Why was I born and what is my purpose in life?" Without purpose there is little hope. Without hope there is really nothing for which to live. So many people these days live an existence that has no hope or purpose. But you don't have to. I am here to tell you that you are here for a reason. You do have a purpose. You were planned, expected and desired by THE God who created the Universe and everything in it. And he wanted you to be a part of His creation. Whoever you are, wherever you come from, whatever your circumstance in life, this very same God knows you, loves you and wanted you before the foundation of the world. And most importantly, He desires to have a personal relationship with you; just you and Him. You don't have to have any special qualities or attributes. All you have to have is a heart that wants to know Him and love Him back. He didn't make you like a puppet on a string, He gave you the ability to choose Him back or choose against Him. Because He loves us, He gives us this choice. He simply loves us and wants us to choose to love Him back. The choice really is ours. Understanding our purpose depends on it. Understandably we want to know what the purpose of our life is. Well, here is the answer. We are here because God wanted us. He wants us. He loves us.

The most amazing aspect I have learned about God is how He loves us. There are no limits to what He will do to make it possible for us to choose Him back out of our desire to do so. The example is what the Bible tells us in the book of Ephesians;

" For by grace you have been saved through faith, and that not of yourselves; it is the gift of God, not of works, lest anyone should boast." Ephesians 2:8-9 (NKJV)

Salvation comes from our acting on the faith that God gives to us by His grace. (grace being undeserved favor) So God has done literally everything necessary for us to have a relationship with Him, but we have to believe or have faith. And we also need to recognize how trust works into this equation.

OK, so how do we choose to have a relationship with God?

Trust in the Lord with all your heart, and lean not on your own understanding; In all your ways acknowledge Him and He shall direct your paths. Proverbs 3:5-6

8 Trust

Trust
 noun: a firm belief in the reliability, truth, ability, or strength of someone or something (Apple dictionary)

Trust is quite possibly the most important aspect of any relationship. Friendships, marriages, parenting, even simple acquaintances are dependent upon this one quality of character. The purposes of this little book are many fold. However, whatever is to be gained by reading this book depends upon trust; not in me as the author, but in you as the reader. My desire is that you trust yourself enough to judge what is contained in this information. Trusting me is more difficult as we don't know each other. We have no history of a relationship upon which to base trust. I do however hope to establish a trust as I believe that it is vitally important.

When I say I want you to trust yourself I am not trying to be condescending, I simply want you to recognize the power that you have in doing so. So many times in our lives we are more or less forced to trust without even considering that we are doing so. And trust is similar to faith in that we exercise it many times without actually thinking about it. For instance; we trusted that the electricity would be on this morning when we awoke. We needed the power to heat the water for our shower, make our coffee, cook our breakfast. We are trusting that if we pay our bill for this service that the people responsible for supplying this product are doing their job to provide it for us. We trust and hope that the other drivers on the road will follow the rules of the road so that our journey to wherever we are going will be uneventful in terms of danger. These are the simple aspects of trust that we tend to take for granted.

There is the "more involved" trust. Like the trust you place in your doctor, surgeon, counselor, etc. You are having to trust these people more than the ordinary aspect of trust. And of course, there are the "intimate relationships" trust. Perhaps you are married or in a close relationship with someone and this demands more trust or better yet a different kind of trust. This kind of trust primarily deals with emotions. Emotions are the life blood of well, life. We all feel something at all times. Too many times we allow our emotions to cloud our judgement. We lose rational thinking and this effects our actions. But this trust is the most important of all trust. The reason being that this trust is tied to our spirit. We are spiritual beings meaning that we combine our thoughts with our emotions. Basically, we listen to our hearts. It's that weird aspect about ourselves that is hard to explain but we understand it innately. We are kind of born with it. Even as infants we naturally express trust in other human beings, especially those who care for us. This trust may also be damaged in this process by those who don't meet our needs from an early age. And as we mature, we are either comfortable trusting others or we are uncomfortable with trusting others, so many of us have to work on the ability to rationally exercise trust.

This is what I want you to exercise, rational trust. No matter who you are, where you come from, what your life experience has been, or what your world view is, you have the ability to place your trust in God. As I stated earlier, the purpose of this book is many fold, meaning that I have a reason for writing it and I believe, I trust that God has a purpose for me writing it. I have long desired to have something written down in this format to give to those people who have questions that don't often get addressed. Personally, I have been asked these questions many times in my life and wished I could go into further detail however usually time constraints or other issues prevented this from happening. Therefore, by the leading of my heart and head, and firm belief that God is leading my feeble attempt, here it is.

I am asking you to trust yourself because that is the best place to start. You don't know me, so asking you to trust that what I present to you in this book as being true is a lot to ask. However, asking God to reveal the truth to you is not. You see, I am sure that everything in this book is not going to be easily understood or believed simply because I wrote it, it's in print, and someone gave it to you or you bought it. Although because the title mentions God, I am confident that you believe in God and desire to know Him in a more personal way. And that in a nutshell is what this book is all about. A personal relationship with THE God who created you and me, and wants us to have that intimate relationship together. It really is a partnership.

Relationship is defined as the state of being connected. Trust is described as a firm belief in the reliability, truth, ability, or strength of someone or something. (dictionary.com) Is it possible to have a fulfilling relationship without trust? Trust is a two-way street meaning that for a relationship to have value both parties must actively engage in practicing this skill. And trust is a skill. Something that we develop in our lives from an early age. We come into this world totally helpless and in need of care. As we grow, we continue to need assistance until we achieve the necessary abilities to care for ourselves. It is during this growth that our understanding of trust is established. Depending on our life experiences we either develop a healthy attitude towards trust, or we develop one that is injured. When you are a baby and in need of complete care and you do not receive it, trust is damaged. And so it is as we mature. When we participate in trusting others and they disappoint us by abusing that trust it is understandable that trust becomes more difficult to exhibit. And for many this is how they view God.

Many people choose to reject God because of their understanding of trust. After all, if He created me then He knew all of the hardships, heartaches, sadness and pain I would endure. How can I trust a God who would do that? What is missing in this rationalization is that we take the choices of others out of the equation. We must recognize that our choices and the choices of others directly and indirectly affect our lives and the lives of others. But if God is all knowing then didn't He know that all of these choices had the capability to bring hardships, heartaches, sadness and pain? IF so, then why did He do it?

Let's follow this line of thinking logically. If we blame God for all the bad things that happen, then should we not praise Him for all the good things also? Consider all of the wonderful aspects of life; Happiness, health, love, etc. If we take away the choices that mankind has made and place everything at God's feet, His responsibility, then of course we could get away with blaming Him for everything. After all, if He started the whole ball rolling then everything is either His guilt or praise, right? We have to acknowledge the simple and yet profound truth that God made choices as well. The rational question is then why did He do it? Why did He create us? The simple truth is this: LOVE. He created us out of love and love is not easy.

What is love? The dictionary defines love as this: an intense feeling of deep affection.(dictionary.com) Now we all know that love can be defined in a myriad of ways so this simple definition falls short. After all, how is it possible that we attach the same word to pizza and children? So, let's just agree that love can be simple or complicated depending on the circumstance. Love also is recognized as an action, not simply an emotion based upon feelings. Action seems to infer that there is choice involved, therefore love can be considered a choice, much like trust.

Trust and love are similar from the standpoint that relationship is vital for both. Our relationship to love and trust are generally learned as a result of interactions with others over the course of our lives. Basically, we trust and love based upon what we have learned and experienced through relating to others.

So how do we truly trust God if we don't have a relationship with Him? Let's go back to the religion discussion. If God created us and knows that man would come up with many different religions why would He just let us flounder around trying to discover which one was the right one for us? Perhaps this is the wrong way to look at it. Remember that God certainly must have known what we would do and it doesn't seem logical that He would not give us a clear way to know Him so it stands to reason that of the multitudes of religions there must be one that is right.

Remember how I told you that before the creation of the world God knew how we would choose? That is true today. The all-knowing God already knows if you will choose Him or reject Him. And even with this knowledge His love for you is unchanging, unending, He chose to create you. He loves you regardless of whether or not you love Him. It's who He is. It's His nature. But also, it is His nature to punish sin, to reject sin and ultimately destroy it. This is why we have the need for a savior. Someone who will accept the punishment of our sin for us. That person is Jesus. I know, for the average person this sounds so foreign. Almost like a fairy tale. How is it possible that God is two beings and yet one, or three beings and yet still only one; that He would choose to become human like us, suffer and die in our place so that we could be with Him forever? The answer requires the wisdom to know where to place your faith and trust.

Delight yourself also in the LORD, And He shall give you the desires of your heart. Psalms 37:4

9 The Great Collaboration

Collaborate

verb: to work, one with another; cooperate usually willingly (dictionary.com)

What is it that we want out of life? Isn't it universal that we all want to feel safe, secure, loved, and have purpose? We all want to feel validated to some degree. We want to establish relationships with friends and family. We long to give and receive love. Did we evolve into this desire? I state definitively no. If you believe in evolution you are missing the boat. That lie is nothing more than a distraction from achieving the aforementioned universal desires. After all, evolution teaches survival of the fittest, the emphasis being on simply surviving. Who among us wants simply to survive? No, life has so much more to offer than simply surviving. Yes, survival is imperative and no doubt a God given trait given to us as well as all of creation, but more important is the relating to another human being, or animal, or plant or anything of which we find worthy. This is God given by design so that we would desire a relationship with others and more importantly with Him. It is born out of His nature, which is love. The Bible tells us that

"He who does not love does not know God, for God is love." 1 John 4:8 NKJV

So, God creates the world and puts us in it, but why? Without a doubt it is because He loves us, He IS love after all and we learn throughout our lives that love isn't love until it is manifested in some form. In other words, it is more of a verb than a noun. Love is proven, more often than not, by action rather than mere words. For example: as we mature in our lives we tend to love more and as a natural progression of this love we want to share it with others. Many times, this takes the form of a lifelong commitment such as marriage. Out of this commitment is the desire to share more love and a natural byproduct, children. Do we desire to have children so that we can be dictators and tyrants over their lives? (Perhaps a teenager reading this may believe so) No, I as a parent desire so much more for my children as I am sure most parents do. We want them safe, secure, loved and filled with purpose. So, the universal desires continue to our offspring. However, during the developmental years of their young lives we find ourselves having to exercise our responsibility as parents and many times direct their actions which, by nature, are contrary to what is best. If you are a parent, and you certainly were a child, you understand what I mean by this. As children we want to make our own decisions even though they may have unintended consequences. So, as parents, out of our love for our children, we discipline them in a way that will help them to make future decisions with better outcomes. That's a nice way of saying that sometimes as children we needed our rear ends smacked, or needed a good bit of time sitting in the corner in order to correct our actions. I know I certainly did, and as an adult and parent, I am thankful that my parents chose to show their love for me in this fashion.

How can we expect anything less of a God who is love and loves us? First and foremost, we must recognize that God has given to us the greatest gift that He could have given to us after the gift of life itself. That is the gift of choice. And this power to make choices in our lives comes with a catch. Choices made always come with consequences and these may be good or bad. I am stating all of this so that we can establish that all the evil in the world is not of God, for which He continuously gets the blame. I can hear you saying; "How could a good and loving God allow these evil, horrific things to happen?" Without choice, we are puppets on strings with every move dictated by the puppet master, and that is not love. Once again let me state as a parent, I certainly dictated many things to my children as they were young and not ready to make certain decisions for themselves. Simply due to their lack of understanding or life experience for that matter, I determined for them many things. No, they could not swim in the deep end of the pool until they had proven their ability to swim in the shallow. No, you can't simply eat desert for every meal. No, you may not shave the dog. Did they gripe and moan? Of course! Did they ask why not? Certainly, and even with reasonable explanation they tended to rebel against my authority as parent and more importantly, guardian of their young inexperienced lives. And there were times that I allowed them to venture into semi dangerous territory so that they could learn through their actions, the unwanted consequences. For example: wanting to ride the bike without the training wheels before I thought that they were ready to do so. This was the tough part of parenting. I didn't want them to suffer the skinned hands and knees, but sometimes learning requires pain, for both me and them. This is the same way it is with God. He loves us and protects us up to a point because He knows that it is imperative that we learn and sometimes that learning comes with pain.

But none of this was a surprise to God. He knew before He spoke the world into existence what the outcome will be. He also knows that this process will involve a lot of painful learning experiences. He gives us choice because He loves us and His desire is that we will choose to love Him back. He lovingly chose to create us knowing that many would not choose to return that love. He created us with a plan in mind for each one of us, knowing us better than we know ourselves, and yet He does not dictate His plan unless we agree to become a partner, or better yet, collaborator in it. And as with any collaboration or partnership there must be a relationship between said persons.

How do we have this relationship with God much less a collaboration with Him? After all He IS God and we are mere mortal beings. As God He must be so far beyond our comprehension or understanding that a real meaningful relationship with Him, especially on an individual level, is impossible. Doesn't He have a Universe to attend to? How can He possibly care about the day to day concerns of someone like me? These are all legitimate questions for our human minds to contemplate based upon who we are. First of all, we must remember that we are NOT God. He created us in His likeness, His image, meaning that we have many traits that He has. And this was done so as to make it possible for us to have a real relationship with Him. Remember, as God, His power is far above our understanding but He does allow us to understand a great deal about Him. And this understanding grows as a direct result of our relationship to Him. Isn't it logical that even in your own life, you get to know someone better by spending more time with them? Having conversations, sharing experiences, etc.? There is but one answer to this question. It is not my opinion but the definitive answer from God Himself.

Jesus.

That one name has the power to evoke both pleasant and unpleasant emotions for many. Have you ever asked yourself why? Perhaps it is because we have a tendency to judge Jesus based upon the actions of those who claim to be His followers. History is replete with misguided actions of which Jesus would not have approved and most assuredly condemned. The reason being that too many have adopted a religion as a societal or cultural item to incorporate into their lives. They may have good intentions, however in order to represent Jesus it is imperative that you know Him personally.

The majority of people don't mind if you proclaim a belief in God, or a "higher power" as is the term used by many. However, when you mention the name of Jesus many of these same people wince. The Bible tells us;

"You believe that there is one God. You do well. Even the demons believe and tremble." James 2:19 (NKJV)

In other words, believing in God is somewhat common throughout the world. Thus, the reason that we have so many religions. Religion is man-made, relationship is God made. This is quite evident throughout the teachings and the life of Jesus. The

Bible also teaches us that Jesus is God as he proclaimed himself to be.

"In the beginning was the Word. And the Word was with God, and the Word was God." John 1:1 (NKJV)

"And the Word became flesh and dwelt among us, and we beheld His glory, the glory as of the only begotten of the Father, full of grace and truth." John1:14 (NKV)

The key to everything in the relationship with God is Jesus. There is no relationship with God without Jesus. There are millions of people, billions of people in the world alive today and also those who lived in the past who truly want and wanted a relationship with God but they would not accept that Jesus was the only way for this to occur. How is this possible you ask? Perhaps they were never taught this. Or if they were taught, they chose to reject it. Which brings us to the question, why would God reject people who wanted to know Him but didn't come through Jesus? We must distinguish that God is not rejecting people, He is rejecting sin. The sad truth is that sin is attached to us. It has been since Adam and Eve took a bite out of the forbidden fruit. And regardless of how well we live our lives, how good our intentions are, there is nothing that we can do to cleanse ourselves of this sin. And this is the reason that God Himself became a man in the form of Jesus, lived a sinless life, and willingly gave His life to pay for our sins.

Let me simply state that this is not my game and not my rules. Thankfully I am not God. Way too big a job for my little brain. God is the one who established His rules. He has told us that Jesus is the only way to Himself. Jesus told us;

" I am the way, the truth, and the life. No one comes to the Father but by me". John 14:6 (NKV)

So, you see He left no wiggle room, or doubt as to whether or not there were many ways to God the Father. He left no other way than through Him. Once again, the choice is up to you. You will choose to believe this or reject it. If you reject it there is no way of having a true relationship with God, only your imagined relationship, not a real one. Now you can have one, many people do. They live their lives based upon their opinions, personal beliefs etc. all to their detriment. God has given a simple and loving way to reach Him. Factually not imagined is the life, death, burial, and resurrection of Jesus. There are many people who reject the actual fact that Jesus was a man who lived approximately 2000 years ago. They reject historical records that were written about Him that aren't even in the Bible. Simple historical data like the kind we read about George Washington, or Abraham Lincoln. Continuing to reject that Jesus is the only way to know God is folly.

The Bible tells us;

"For many are called, but few are chosen" Matthew 22:14 (NKJV)

God is calling you to Himself. If you answer, you are chosen. Why are we here? What is our purpose? Is there a God? Why did He create us? Why does He allow so much evil and pain in the world? Why should He care about ME? These are questions that all of us wrestle with at one time or another in the course of our lives. The answers are out there, when we find them, we begin to understand this wonderful adventure called life. I have found them and I want to share them with you, for one reason, the same reason we all were created, love. Because I love you. The love of God who created us all, flows through me and reaches out to you. This very God who knows everything, every molecule, in every part of His creation, loves us more than we can begin to imagine. He is concerned with every aspect of our lives. He knows us better than we know ourselves. And He wants us to know Him back. But it is our choice.

Let's recap what we have thus far discussed. There is a God who created everything, most importantly he created you out of his desire. The God who created the universe and everything in it wanted you. He planned you, designed you, and placed you in His creation at exactly the right time in which He wanted you to be. This was done out of love because God is love and He loves like no one else ever has or ever will. He wants you to choose to make Him Lord of your life and to collaborate with Him regarding your life. Now when I say collaborate with God, I am explaining that He has a perfect plan for your life but we all know that we don't live in a perfect world. However, He has the capability, power, and desire to adjust His plan according to your actions. Depending upon your willingness to collaborate with Him regarding your life the consequences may be beneficial or detrimental. And don't misunderstand me here. Becoming a child of God is the greatest experience anyone may have but it is in no way a rose garden, or a life without problems. However, when you choose to follow Christ, to be a Born-Again Believer in Him, the Holy Spirit comes to live in you, He regenerates your dead sinful spirit and gives you new life, eternal life.

"Therefore, if anyone is in Christ, he is a new creation; old things have passed away; behold, all things have become new." 2 Corinthians 5:17 (NKJV)

Furthermore, He gives you a promise to never leave you or forsake you.

"And I give them eternal life, and they shall never perish; neither shall anyone snatch them out of My hand. My Father, who has given them to Me, is greater than all; and no one is able to snatch them out of My Father's hand. I and My Father are one." John 10:28-30 (NKJV)

He promises us peace in the midst of suffering. Jesus said;

"These things I have spoken to you, that in Me you may have peace. In the world you will have tribulation; but be of good cheer, I have overcome the world." John 16:33 (NKJV)

Some people have preconceived ideas about Jesus, about religion in general. This is understandable especially in this day and age. There are so many religions and each one proclaims itself to be the "right" one. So, it is important to state again and understand that religion is a man-made thing. That's right, man-made. Relationship is God made. Now understand that I am a follower of Jesus so I am labeled a Christian. And this label describes the religion of Christianity. But in truth, God only cares about our relationship to Him, not the labels we attach for our own self-worth. Being a part of a religion and knowing God personally are two different things. Religions tend to have organizations and rules and regulations of which I am sure you are well aware. Once again, I will say they are a man-made thing. Many designed to tell us that there are ways to gain God's favor, approval, acceptance, but that is not the way God works.

"Come to Me, all you who labor and are heavy laden, and I will give you rest. Take My yoke upon you and learn from Me, for I am gentle and lowly in heart, and you will find rest for your souls. For My yoke is easy and My burden is light." Matthew 11:28-30 (NKJV)

For those who may not be aware of what a "yoke" is let me explain. A yoke is the leather or wooden neck piece put on beasts of burden such as oxen or horses pulling a cart. It generally has leather straps or rope attached to it that allows the driver to pull in a direction for the beast to follow. Jesus is saying that as we come to Him and allow Him to direct our lives that He is not a hard driver, pulling hard and yanking the ropes to direct your life, He is saying that His direction is easy to follow and the burden of the cart is not weighted down so heavy it is hard to move. No, He is saying that with Him as the driver, and you as the one pulling the load that your collaboration together for the direction of your life will bring peace to your soul.

He desires for us to live an abundant life, and I don't mean abundant in the aspect of material possessions. God has always cared more about our spiritual life than our physical prosperity. In fact, He recognizes that we tend to get distracted by physical things that keep us from missing the more important spiritual ones. Perhaps this is what Jesus was talking about when the rich young ruler came to Him asking what he could do to obtain eternal life.

But the young man was too attached to earthly things to abandon them and follow Jesus. The famous verse associated with this interaction shows us how difficult it is to be concerned with our relationship to God when we possess too much of the world's goods. The book of Matthew gives us the story of Jesus who was approached by a wealthy man:

Now behold, one came and said to Him, "Good Teacher, what good thing shall I do that I may have eternal life?"

So He said to him, "Why do you call Me good? No one is good but One, that is, God. But if you want to enter into life, keep the commandments."

He said to Him, "Which ones?"

Jesus said, "'You shall not murder,' 'You shall not commit adultery,' 'You shall not steal,' 'You shall not bear false witness,' Honor your father and your mother,' and, You shall love your neighbor as yourself.'"

The young man said to Him, "All these things I have kept from my youth. What do I still lack?"

Jesus said to him, "If you want to be perfect, go, sell what you have and give to the poor, and you will have treasure in heaven; and come, follow Me."

But when the young man heard that saying, he went away sorrowful, for he had great possessions.

Then Jesus said to His disciples, "Assuredly, I say to you that it is hard for a rich man to enter the kingdom of heaven. And again I say to you, it is easier for a camel to go through the eye of a needle than for a rich man to enter the kingdom of God." Matthew 19:16-24 (NKJV)

"But those who desire to be rich fall into temptation and a snare, and into many foolish and harmful lusts which drown men in destruction and perdition. For the LOVE of money is a root of all kinds of evil, for which some have strayed from the faith in their greediness, and pierced themselves through with many sorrows." 1 Timothy 6:10 (NKJV)

Now don't misunderstand what I am trying to relate to you. Money is not the problem and having a lot of it is by no means a sin. Jesus was simply trying to help us understand the temptation that goes along with too many earthly possessions. They tend to demand more of our time and loyalty than the more important relationship with God. Money in and of itself is a tool.

We need to establish the fact that we should NEVER take God out of the equation. When we are trying to figure something out, or determine a direction, or answer simple or complicated questions it is always best to remember that there is a God who is sovereign and has a plan. He always has answers however, sometimes answering those questions we pose may not be the best direction at the time. What I mean is that so many people say that they have prayed and asked God for something and He hasn't answered their prayer yet. I have learned that God always has an answer, that answer may be "wait" or "no, not right now" or "yes". But it is only when God gives the "yes" that many people mistakenly believe that He has "answered" their prayer.

Perhaps I should talk a little bit about prayer at this point. I have taken for granted that most people understand what prayer is. Prayer is simply talking to God. Yeah, I know that we talked earlier about there not being any person 'in the flesh" that is God walking around here on earth but let's recognize again that we are mostly spiritual beings made in the image of God who is mostly spirit Himself. And I say, "mostly," because remember, Jesus is a part of the Trinity Godhead and He became flesh so as to relate to us in a manner that we could better understand the whole spiritual aspect of who we are. There is a spiritual aspect to prayer as it is directly connected to your heart. God knows the condition of your heart and will listen when your heart is yielded to wanting to be in connection with Him. The Bible tells us;

"...For the LORD does not see as man sees; for man looks at the outward appearance, but the LORD looks at the heart."1 Samuel 16:7 (NKJV)

Does that make sense?

Let me try to give you an analogy that may make better sense. Do you own a pet? A cat or a dog or maybe a bird? You have a way of communicating with them, don't you? Certain words you have used over and over that they understand the meaning. When I see if my dogs need or want to go outside, I ask them if they need to go "hurry". It's a word that I learned from a friend of mine years ago that he used for his little dog. He would go outside with the dog and continue to say, "hurry" so as to encourage the dog to use the bathroom so they could go back inside, especially in cold weather. So, the dog got used to the term and it meant something. Has your dog ever gotten into your trash can and strewn trash all over the floor? I am sure the dog doesn't understand exactly what you are saying but the tone of your voice when you are mad that they have made a mess certainly communicates a message. But imagine if you could figure out a way to communicate EXACTLY what you wanted to tell your dog? How would you go about that? What would be the best way in which to do that? You would BECOME a dog! Then you could communicate in the language of the dog, there would be no problem because you are one of them!

I know that may be a poor analogy but understand that before God ever created the universe and this world and especially mankind, He knew that He would become flesh and dwell among us. He knew that He would do this to communicate face to face the plan that God has had all along. Jesus became a man to help us to learn how to communicate better with the Father and also most importantly to repair the connection that was lost in the Garden of Eden when Adam and Eve chose to disobey and cripple our relationship with God.

Let's talk again about something that I am sure you have asked yourself. If God has a perfect plan then why isn't everything perfect? Why is there so much pain and suffering in the world? If He wanted me and planned me and placed me here in the world but I am born with physical deformities, or addicted to crack, or psychologically disturbed how can that be considered perfect? These are all legitimate and reasonable questions. And there are answers and I will try to give you the logical track that may at times seem illogical. The first thing we must remember is to never take God out of the equation. What I mean is that we can never determine an outcome to any given situation and not understand that He does in fact enter into the equation at some point.

Consider a math equation for example. $1 + 4 + 0 = 5$, right? So, what is the point of putting the zero in the equation? $1 + 4 = 5$ is the same thing, right? The point I am making is that even when it looks as if nothing or zero is not a necessary part of the equation sometimes it can make a huge difference. Change the addition to multiplication and see what I mean. $1 \times 4 \times 0 = 0$. God is in everything and yet He chooses not to act in all situations. He can stop accidents from happening. He can keep children from being born with birth defects. He can heal or prevent disease. Then why doesn't He? My answer to this question is not a simple explanation. Although He can do all of these things, He chooses not to and yet He also chooses to, depending on the situation. God's ways and our ways are not the same. I know that sounds like a cop out rationalization but it kind of answers the question. Not being God, it is hard to fathom all of the variables that go into the decisions He makes. We first must recognize that He is perfect and doesn't make mistakes and that alone is almost impossible to comprehend. His decisions are based upon knowing everything that there is to know about the situation. What every outcome would be if any particular variable was changed even in the slightest. This is where faith and trust in Him are of vital importance.

I will try to explain it using some examples from movies that have been made. Did you ever see the movie "Back to the Future"? In the movie there was discussion about making sure not to change anything when going back to the past because it may in effect change the future. Marty went back in the past and messed up the chance meeting that his parents had met upon and inadvertently changed the future where he was no longer a part. (good thing we can't really time travel back into the past huh?!) The point being that one little change in a situation may affect a great deal of events in the future.

Did you happen to see the movies "The Avengers Infinity War and End Game"? This whole series of movies which are fantasy, and fictional to be clear, was fascinating to me and yet possibly without even knowing or intending to the writer's plot had such religious connotations in them. The Avengers were trying to defeat an egomaniacal villain named Thanos who sought to destroy half of the universal population. An Avenger named Dr. Strange was in control of the "infinity time stone" which allowed him to go back in time or into the future. Thanos needed this stone in order to achieve his diabolical scheme. There is a scene in "Infinity War" where it looks as if Dr. Strange is having some sort of break down but what he is actually doing is going forward in time and seeing every variable in every possible future situation to see if there was a way to defeat Thanos. When asked by Iron Man if there was such scenario, Dr. Strange replied that after looking at millions of possible scenarios that there was only one in which they win.

The point I am poorly attempting to make is that it's hard to grasp that God really can do what Dr. Strange was doing in the movie. Of course, the movie is a fictional fantasy because we don't have the power to see into the future, much less change it. But God CAN! He can look into the future and He does already see every scenario in our lives and how they will play out, but He also has the power to inject Himself at any time into that future. That means that He can change the future according to His will and yet He also considers our choices when doing so. And thus, the reason that before the creation of the Universe Jesus knew that He would have to sacrifice Himself as a man in order to save us. His love is so great that He willingly chose to meet the required payment for our sin in order for us to have an eternity with Him and not out of fear of going to Hell, but out of our choosing to love Him back.

So, if you have followed me this far, as hard as it may be to comprehend, God has planned everything to fit ultimately into His will. Notice that I said, ultimately. We must remember that God's will is not always done here on this earth because of the choice's mankind has made. Our rebellion against God from the beginning has caused a chain reaction that has affected the whole of creation. I certainly wasn't there in the Garden of Eden to disobey God face to face and neither were you, but there is no denying that we choose to do so now. But also remember in all of that planning God has included His grace and mercy that gives us what we need to live life in this fallen world, but not just live, live abundantly.

God knew Lucifer would fall, He knew Adam and Eve would disobey, He knew that the history of mankind would be filled with atrocities against itself. He knew that hatred would fill the hearts of so many and even though He knew that the majority of the people He lovingly created would reject Him, He still chose to create because He doesn't just love, He IS love. The creation of us is the most natural outpouring of His nature, almost as if He could not stop himself from creating us.

Scripture is given by inspiration of God, and is profitable for doctrine, for reproof, for correction, for instruction in righteousness.

2 Timothy 3:16

10 The Bible, God's Word

We hold these truths to be self-evident, that all men are created equal, that they are endowed by their Creator with certain unalienable Rights, that among these are Life, Liberty and the pursuit of Happiness.

These words written over 200 years ago by man with a desire to establish a nation of freedom, along with the vast responsibility it entails, were in no doubt inspired by God. The phrase unalienable rights meaning, not transferable to another or not capable of being taken away or denied is appropriate when we consider God and his design of humanity. God has created this universe and determined that the most important aspect of it is mankind. It is truly incomprehensible to understand the complexity of all of creation therefore it is imperative that we focus on what we are able to comprehend and hopefully understand; That being the miracle of human life.

In consideration of our belief in a creator let us rationally set aside the debate of evolution until later. Science has determined that the complexity of this creation demands an intelligence that has planned, organized, and set into motion life itself. The mechanism of a simple cell substantiates and affirms intelligent design and therefore reasonable logic demands recognition of a creator. And because there is a creator, all of creation cries out for recognition and praise to be given to this creator and that most assuredly, if not predominately, includes mankind. That would be you and me.

So, we believe that we were created by an all-powerful being of which we have a limited comprehension and understanding. However, even in our limited understanding we still should recognize that there is a plan, a design, that must have been perfect in its inception. But look around, any fool can perceive the imperfection that is evident in this creation. So, what happened? How is it possible that an all-powerful, all knowing God who is incontrovertibly perfect, create an imperfect world, and perhaps more importantly how does mankind fit into this picture? I'm glad you asked!

We live in an amazing day and age full of information. Answers to questions that have baffled generations are being answered today. The cumulative knowledge of the entire world multiplies exponentially each year. And the thirst for knowledge never seems to be filled. However, there are questions that are universal and continuing in every generation. "Why am I here? Where did I come from? Is there a God?" For many these questions are satisfied in the form of a world view that includes a faith or religious belief system and yet how can they all be true? So many of the religions of the world are contradictory to each other. Some examples are; there is reincarnation where when you die you come back to life in another form of life to better yourself in preparation for the ultimate destination of perfection and an existence in total bliss. There is the belief that this life is all that there is, once you die, you no longer exist, there is no afterlife.

Some believe that there is a god but that you cannot know him personally because he is too great for our minds to fathom and yet he is involved in every aspect of life on earth. For this belief system there is an afterlife but it is based upon this god's determination of where you will spend it. A capricious god that allows for no security or assurance of paradise except through the sacrifice of one's self in an act of war killing yourself and others who don't believe exactly as you do. Interestingly the majority of these religions that believe in a god or gods, determine the afterlife experience based upon one's worthiness and their performance in life and often fail to answer the simple question of why was I created. And these are just a few of the over 4000 known religions in our world today.

And this is where the Bible comes in. It is a supernatural book written over thousands of years by over 40 different people and yet it has one theme throughout. It is the story of God's relationship to man and His plan for mankind and is filled with people and stories and truth and so much that the average reader misses without the assistance of the Holy Spirit of God. I am not a theologian. There are no big initials at the end of my name such as PhD or MA etc. I am just a simple man who has experienced extraordinary things. So, if that can sink in, I think you will better understand where I am coming from.

"In the beginning God created the Heavens and the Earth". Genesis 1:1 (NKJV)

If you accept that this is true then everything else is secondary. What I mean is that you have to believe that God created you and has a purpose for you in order for you to have a relationship with

Him. But what exactly does a relationship with God look like? How does it function? It's not like He is a physical being walking around here on earth that I can go to and ask advice or expect some tangible evidence of His existence. It is extremely frustrating in this day and age to try to believe that I can communicate with the God of the Universe, it is even more difficult to believe that He could possibly care about or even become involved in the things that I care about or concern me.

So, let's just look at the issue of God rationally and logically. If there is a God, and I am a firm believer that there is because I know Him personally, then it makes sense that He is far beyond our normal comprehension of all that He is. So, it is a futile endeavor to attempt to explain all of God and basically impossible. However, there is a great deal about God that we can understand based upon personal experience and history. Historically we have what is known as the Holy Bible. There are those who argue that the Bible was written by men so how can it be of God much less a message system that God wants us to use for direction in our lives? Remember what I stated earlier, never take God out of the equation. When we attempt to answer questions that seem valid, we must remember that we are working from a limited inventory of knowledge. And also remember that God isn't an idiot and certainly has taken everything into account regarding the way in which He wanted to get the message to us. The History of the Bible itself is fascinating. How over thousands of years Holy inspired writings became scriptures that have given us insight into the heart and mind of the creator of the Universe. Of course, that is not just my personal opinion but is shared by millions of others throughout the world. I would encourage you to study the origins of the Bible for yourself and recognize the amazing power of God to put this work that is considered to be His word, in easy access to anyone in the western world.

Let me pause a moment here to ask that you continue to read this with an open mind. I refer to the Bible quite frequently and I understand that there will certainly be those who read this that don't necessarily believe that the Bible is something to be trusted. After all it was written by men, right? That is why from the beginning I am telling you that at its foundation, at the core of your belief system it has to be your choice. You are the one who makes the choice, not me, not your parents, not your employer, your wife, your husband. No, you must make the choice regarding your relationship to God. But don't you want to have as much information as you can to make a wise choice? The Bible is considered by millions, no billions, to be God's word to mankind so let's not discount it. There are certainly many reasons to believe that it is a message system from God.

The Bible we have today and its many translations extend from the King James Version that was completed in 1604. This is a work that translates into the "kings English" from the Hebrew of the Old Testament and the Greek of the New Testament.

The Bible is just a book to those who don't know God. To His children it is His word. One of the His chosen ways to get His message across to mankind. It truly is a magnificent work even to the non-believer. It is a book compiled of smaller "books" and is also known as "scripture". It is 66 books written by 40 authors over thousands of years. It is filled with prophecy or as I have heard that described as "pre written history," which is one of the defining characteristics of this particular "Holy book". Now remember there are literally thousands of religions in our world today. Many with "Holy books" claiming to be ancient and true.

There are many that are ancient but not true. One of the reasons we can place our faith and trust in the Bible is because of this prophecy or pre written history.

"Down through history, God provided us a roadmap. He foretold various signs and conditions through His prophets. These prophets spoke of things that mankind should watch for so that the Messiah would be recognized and believed. These signs or prophecies were given to us in the Old Testament. The Old Testament is the part of the Bible written before Jesus was born. Its writings were completed in 450 B.C. The Old Testament, written hundreds of years before Jesus' birth contains over 300 prophecies that Jesus fulfilled through His life, death, and resurrection.

Mathematically speaking, the odds of anyone fulfilling this amount of prophecy are staggering. Mathematicians put it this way:

1 person fulfilling 8 prophecies: 1 in 100,000,000,000,000,000, 1 person fulfilling 48 prophecies: 1 chance in 10 to the 157th power; 1 person fulfilling 300+ prophecies Only Jesus! (www1.cbn.com/biblestudy/biblical-prophecies-fulfilled-by-jesus)

The reason God gave us this work called the Bible authored by so many different people over such a long period of time is because He wanted to show us without a doubt that He is THE God, not A god. Being THE God and creator of time itself He is outside of the dimension of time.

Time has been proven through scientific method to be a physical property. It is a dimension that God created for mankind. He knew in His infinite wisdom that man would need time. It's as simple as knowing that we were created, that we have not always been because we are not God. There is scientific evidence that proves time to be a physical property or dimension. Once again let me point to an excellent video on YouTube that describes this concept and scientific aspect so much better than I can here. (https://youtu.be/rshwuQVz_ZO) Chuck Missler YouTube "Time is a Physical Property") Einstein suggested this to be true and subsequently through many scientific methods it has been proven.

You see God being outside of time already has seen what is going to happen, what has happened and what is happening now; Thus, His description of Himself to Moses as the I AM. If we relate God to time, everything is happening now for God. He sees what is in our future and has given bits and pieces of it in prophecy to show to man that He is THE God, not a God and not an imaginary man-made being. This is why the Bible is such an important book. In fact, it is more than a book, it is a supernatural message sent by God for us to know that He is the one and only true God.

He actually resides outside of time and inside of time to communicate with us. He is not bound by time like we are. We relate to time because we can understand it. We were born, we live, we die; Past, present, future. Three aspects or attributes of the same one thing, time. The best explanation I have ever heard is this.

Imagine you are sitting on the sidewalk in Main Street USA waiting on a parade. You see the floats and marching bands coming from down the street (future), then they pass in front of you (present), then they pass on down the street (past). You only can see what you can see relative to where you are sitting etc. God is in a helicopter hovering over the parade and can see the entire thing at once. He knows when everything is happening. He sees the staging area where the bands and floats are gathering together preparing to take their place in the parade. He could tell you when the Snoopy balloon will be coming by, when the marching band will be right in front of you because He sees it all, He is not limited by just what is in front of you or what you can see. He sees where the parade ends, the area where they break down the floats and disband the balloons and the marching bands.

This is why the Bible is the only book by which to know the Truth of God. It is filled with prophecy. These prophecies, or pre written history, are snippets of time taken from the future so that we can know that He is THE God. The one who created time. I can't talk about God without referencing the Bible because this is the book from which we learn so much about Him. It's kind of a jumping off point so to speak. It is a reference guide in which I have placed my trust and it has never failed me; Not only me but literally billions of others over the years. And understand that it is a tool that helps us to achieve the purpose for which it was written, to help us have a relationship to God.

Quoting the great preacher Reverend Voddie Baucham Jr.;

"Mainly the reason I believe that the Bible is the Word of God is because it's a reliable collection of historical documents written by eye witnesses during the lifetime of other eyewitnesses written by other eyewitnesses. They report supernatural events that took place in fulfillment of specific prophecies and claim that their writings are Devine rather than human in origin. There is no other so called 'Holy Book' that comes close to any one of those attributes. I believe that God created the world in six literal days, I have no problem believing that He can create a fish to be used to carry a man about. That gives me no pause whatever because we are not talking about some figment of my imagination, we are talking about the God who put the stars in space. We are talking about the God who said, 'Let there be...' and it was. We're talking about the God who created the sun that is beaming down on me right now. I have no problem whatsoever believing Jonah. You can't say on one hand the Bible is a great book and then on the other that it lies. Great books don't lie. Great books don't claim to be one thing when in fact they are another so people either have to admit that they do not believe the Bible is a not a great book or they have to acknowledge what the Bible says and the claims that the Bible makes. But you cannot have it both ways."

One of the many reasons that I am writing this book is because I have come into contact with many people who in my opinion miss out on the most wonderful aspect of life. Having a personal, meaningful relationship with God has been the most amazing aspect of my life. And the sad thing is that those who have been taught, wrongly so, that the only way to do that is conforming to a certain set of tenets or rules in order to do so. Now don't get me wrong, God certainly has rules but it is important to understand why.

As a Nation we have established laws. We also have what is defined as morality that is established by what society deems as acceptable behavior for its people. We gained wisdom from God and His word to establish laws; As an example, consider the famous Ten Commandments. They all are about us and protecting us, wanting what is best for us whether we like it or not. The first three would appear to be about Him. However, look closely to the intention.

And God spoke all these words, saying:

"I Am the LORD your God, who brought you out of the land of Egypt, out of the house of bondage.

"You shall have no other gods before Me.

"You shall not make for yourself a carved image—any likeness of anything that is in heaven above, or that is in the earth beneath, or that is in the water under the earth; you shall not bow down to them nor serve them. For I, the LORD your God, am a jealous God, visiting the iniquity of the fathers upon the children to the third and fourth generations of those who hate Me, but showing mercy to thousands, to those who love Me and keep My commandments.

"You shall not take the name of the LORD your God in vain, for the LORD will not hold him guiltless who takes His name in vain.

"Remember the Sabbath day, to keep it holy. Six days you shall labor and do all your work, but the seventh day is the Sabbath of the LORD your God. In it you shall do no work: you, nor your son, nor your daughter, nor your male servant, nor your female servant, nor your cattle, nor your stranger who is within your gates. For in six days the LORD made the heavens and the earth, the sea, and all that is in them, and rested the seventh day. Therefore, the LORD blessed the Sabbath day and hallowed it.

"Honor your father and your mother, that your days may be long upon the land which the LORD your God is giving you.

"You shall not murder.

"You shall not commit adultery.

"You shall not steal.

"You shall not bear false witness against your neighbor.

"You shall not covet your neighbor's house; you shall not covet your neighbor's wife, nor his male servant, nor his female servant, nor his ox, nor his donkey, nor anything that is your neighbor's." Exodus 20:1-17 (NKJV)

Now let me give you a breakdown of what I believe these commandments intend to relate to us, so that they are beneficial to us in our daily lives.

Number 1: "I am the Lord thy God; you shall have no other gods before me." Well, that one is pretty self-explanatory, He is God, the one and only and He doesn't want us to mistakenly follow some pretend god when He knows that He is the one and only. Otherwise we could get into a heap of trouble following some false god. So, when God has said He is a jealous God, He means that He doesn't want us following lies. He is not jealous in the way we think of jealousy, as in "how dare they like some other god more than me". Nope, He is THE God, pretty sure He isn't intimidated by pretenders, just doesn't like their knack of harming us with their lies and deception. So, in effect the first commandment really isn't not about Him, but about us. Have you ever thought of it that way? Well, hold on,

Number 2: "Thou shalt not make unto thyself any graven image." That is an unusual term, of course that is from the King James version of the Bible. The New King James Version is what I quote from the most because of the "Thee's and Thou's and words like Graven which is changed to "carved" in the NKJV.

Graven image means an idol. The Bible tells us that God is Spirit and making a graven image of a spirit seems to me to be difficult. But the purpose here is that when we make a physical representation of something that is not physical, i.e. Love, we tend to worship that representation instead of the actual thing itself. I believe God was warning us of making idols that even though well intentioned to represent Him, do not in fact represent Him. More importantly they tend to distract us from the most important aspect of knowing Him, and distract from our spiritual connection with Him. Are you following me? There is that word again, distraction. God knows how easily distracted we can become regarding anything. Worshipping an idol even though we might believe that it represents Him is in fact a distraction from the true relationship that He desires for us to have with Him. We tend to feel like in order to get closer to God or connect with Him we have to go to a church building, synagogue, mosque, chapel, wherever there are symbols of Him. Sadly, churches are places that have these graven images too. Haven't you seen the large Crucifix, many carvings of Saints, or the European Jesus picture hanging in a church? You know the one that has the handsome Jesus with the pale white skin and the silky brown hair? Come on, Jesus was a Jewish Middle Easterner, He of course probably had olive or dark color skin, and even the Bible describes him as not anything special as far as appearance goes. God doesn't want us to get caught up or distracted by the physical when the spiritual is the most important. Ok that was number two, still about us.

Number 3: "Thou shalt not take the name of the Lord thy God in vain." To many people this means that we shouldn't say; "oh my God", or "my God", or the biggest one "God dam*it". Once again, it's not about God as much as it is about us. This commandment is about the representation of God. If you will, the ambassadorship of who He is to others. God is saying that if you are His, you take or accept the responsibility of representing Him. Similar to when a wife takes the last name of her husband when they are married. She now represents him and his family name. Also the phrase "You shall not take" Exodus 20:7 (NKJV) comes from the Hebrew root word of nasa' which describes it as; to carry, to bear, and accept, to name a few of the descriptions (Strongs Concordance H5375) It's not about the words themselves but about the attitude that results in action. In other words, He doesn't want us to take our relationship with Him lightly or in vain. The term "in vain" comes from the Hebrew word shav' which describes it as; emptiness, worthlessness, nothingness. (Strongs Concordance H7723) This would instruct us to understand the importance of our representation of Him; so again, it's about our actions and not simply the words. After all, is God really His name? There are in fact many people who use the term God and yet are not even calling on the one and only True God. The Bible even tells us that pronouncing His name is impossible. Perhaps this is why Jesus taught us to refer to Him as Father, or Abba which means "daddy". Once again, we tend to get caught up in the distraction rather than the original intent. Taking God's name in vain is in fact misrepresenting who and what He is and should not be a part of who we are as ambassadors of His truth. Now don't get me wrong, these phrases "my God" etc. tend to offend many people and why do that when it's not necessary? But the focus should once again be on the Spiritual connection to God the Father, how do you represent your relationship to Him? What IS your relationship to Him? That is what this whole book is about, after all it's your choice as whether or not you even have one. He certainly desires one with you! Let's continue.

Number 4: "Remember the sabbath day to keep it holy." Well, boy is this one ever screwed up. But leave it to us to replace one day with another. Jesus was a Jew. Labels, hate em but they are necessary. So the Jewish religion which was really just the pathway that God set forth for mankind but we have to label it, is how God established himself, or I should say, set Himself apart, from all the other religions that had begun since Adam and Eve were kicked out of the Garden for disobedience. They have scripture that is thousands of years old, considered the word of God because most importantly it is full of prophecy. Now remember prophecy is "pre written" history. In other words, THE God who is outside of time, can see all of time at the same time. Did you get that? God already knows everything that is going to happen and already has happened. But we on the other hand live day to day. We are limited by time and space. We have boundaries and we need them to function in this limited world. Of course, God is perfect, doesn't "guess" at anything, gets nothing wrong, and has a plan for it all. I know, big concept but stay with me. So, God gives the Jewish people, also known as the "chosen people," this scripture including what we are talking about here, the ten commandments. (understand that the term "chosen people" is a term used to describe the people that God set apart to show to the world who He is, that He is the one and only True God) So the sabbath is the seventh day of the week, or on our calendar it is Saturday. However, the Christian community in its zeal to show authority for God, well-intentioned but poorly executed, established the first day of the week, Sunday as "the Lord's day" basically replacing the Sabbath. However, God wasn't surprised at this, as He never is, and uses Sunday as one of the most spiritual days in the Christian community where worshipers gather and praise and fellowship. Understanding God's dealings with mankind is one of the neatest aspects of a personal relationship with Him. According to our willingness to know and commune with Him, He reveals Himself constantly regardless of how we tend to screw things up.

Back to the purpose of the "Sabbath". God created the universe in six days according to the Bible and He rested on the seventh. Think about that for a moment. God rested. I don't know about you but even in my limited mind I can't think of a reason THE God would ever need rest. I mean, He is God, all powerful, all knowing etc. . SO the rest thing is once again, for US. We need the boundary of rest. We need it for physical reasons but more importantly we need it for spiritual reasons. We need time to regroup, rethink, relax, pause a moment and focus on the most important aspects of life, relationships. Especially those of us who are His children, born again of His Sprit, need time together for this worship, fellowship, sharing and learning from other believers. So even though we screwed up the actual "Sabbath" day, we still set aside a day in which to do what God knew we needed to do. As you grow in your relationship with God you will find His ability to work good out of bad is amazing and comforting. But once again the question remains, what kind of relationship do you have with God? Do you have a relationship with THE God, not a god of your choosing. There is a difference, but He has given you the choice.

The rest of the commandments are pretty much easy to understand as they deal with relatively rational morality.

Number 5: "Honor thy Father and Mother that thy days may be long upon the earth which the Lord thy God has given thee." Respect and trust are important aspects of all relationships; But especially your Father and Mother, the ones responsible for the physical action that made you. And regardless of whether or not they are your biological parents, God has placed them in your life for a purpose, a reason in His plan for your life. It is the first place you learn trust, faith, love and respect which will be vital in all relationships in your life.

Number 6: "Don't kill or better yet don't commit murder." Because life is sacred.

Number 7: "Don't commit adultery." Once again respect and trust but sex outside of marriage is called fornication and with someone other than your spouse is adultery and is sin. Although in today's morally corrupt mentality it's like breathing in and breathing out, and it destroys so many relationships, especially marriage. And in the covenant of marriage you make a commitment. Adhering to the commitments you make throughout life are the stuff of which your character is built. Sex is a beautiful creation by God as a gift for His children with the intent of procreation. This is quite possibly the area of life where Satan does the most damage with the intent to destroy the family unit established by God.

Number 8: "Don't steal." Again, respect and trust regarding material things.

Number 9: "Don't bear false witness against your neighbor." In other words, don't lie, especially about someone else; Once again, relationship destroyer.

Number 10: "Don't covet." Meaning don't spend your life desiring you had what someone else has, wishing away your life instead of working with God to achieve His purposes for you.

And this is just the ten commandments. The Bible, God's message system to us is full of stories, history, examples, and rules that we are given the choice to believe and apply to our lives or reject as simply literary gobbledygook. History has shown that so many, and this includes me, the benefits experienced from earnestly seeking to know God personally and using the Bible as a guidebook for life. But the most important aspect of the entire Bible is that it is a story of redemption. The redemption of mankind which is necessary for us to have a relationship with God. And the Bible is all about the Redeemer who is Jesus. I encourage you to read the first four books of the New Testament for yourself, they are known as "The Gospels" or "Good News" and are about the life and ministry of Jesus given from four men from different perspectives. However, there is no doubt that you will come to understand who He is and what He did during His life and ministry. He is in the Old Testament concealed and in the New

Testament revealed. An amazing gift of Love from THE God who
IS LOVE.

You believe that there is one God. You do well. Even the demons believe, and tremble! James 2:19

11 The Religion of Evolution

I love a good spirited debate. I enjoy teaching as well as learning from someone else who is as passionate about any given subject and willing to defend their point of view. However, there comes a point when debate is futile, it is like trying to dress a pig. You inevitably are going to get dirty and it's going to annoy the pig. This is how I feel about debating evolution. However, it is a necessary discussion for many who have accepted this teaching without giving it its rational, logical examination. So hopefully without getting into too long of a drawn-out discussion let's touch on this subject. It is rational to believe that this earth upon which we live, and the Universe surrounding us was created. The intricate design that science has discovered about the Universe as well as the Human being tends to squash the evolution theory. And let me repeat that important word that is often left out these days, THEORY. The mechanics of the cells within our bodies speak of design not happenstance. Logic would suggest that even if you say that all of this happened over billions of years that the design in DNA is much too complex for it to have merely happened by chance.

Now for our purposes, let us establish which types of evolution there are; Microevolution is defined as: "evolutionary change within a species or small group of organisms, especially over a short period." (Apple Dictionary) Take notice of the designation "within a species" that generally occur gradually.

Mutations that may "evolve" over time due to environment or other factors however, the microevolution is ALWAYS within the species. I firmly believe this as there is empirical evidence proving it.

Macroevolution is defined as: "major evolutionary transition from one type of organism to another occurring at the level of species and higher taxa." (dictionary.com) This means a transformation from one organism to another type of organism. In other words changing from one species to another, but of course over time, a lot of time. And although there is a lot of theoretical evidence, much of which has been questioned and proven false, there is no empirical evidence. Therefore, I don't subscribe to the theory of macroevolution because I know the God who created me personally and I believe His word that tells me the I was created. However, simple logic also would give me pause regardless of how many estimated years are explained away and used to confuse and deceive us. Creation which denotes design is simple, logical, and rational. But the choice is yours. What do you believe?

There is one indisputable fact in this adventure called life and that is the fact that no one gets out alive. We are all destined to die, bite the mop, take a dirt nap, become worm food, push up daisies… you get the picture. The one thing that has always bothered me in the attempt to circumvent this or avoid it is the simple question; why do we die? I mean in this day and age with the amazing advancements in science and knowledge we have learned how to extend life, give a better quality of life, but we don't seem to be addressing the elephant in the room. Why do we die?

In the beginning God created Adam and Eve and they were perfect and without any separation from a Holy and perfect God. And He gave them a choice. They choose to rebel against Him because the liar Satan deceived them into making that choice. Satan deceived Eve by coaxing her to doubt God.

"Now the serpent was more cunning than any beast of the field which the LORD God had made. And he said to the woman, 'Has God indeed said, "You shall not eat of every tree of the garden?"'

And the woman said to the serpent, 'We may eat the fruit of the trees of the garden; but of the fruit of the tree which is in the midst of the garden, God has said, "You shall not eat it, nor shall you touch it, lest you die."

Then the serpent said to the woman, 'You will not surely die. For God knows that in the day you eat of it your eyes will be opened, and you will be like God, knowing good and evil.'

So, when the woman saw that the tree was good for food, that it was pleasant to the eyes, and a tree desirable to make one wise, she took of its fruit and ate. She also gave to her husband with her, and he ate. Then the eyes of both of them were opened, and they knew that they were naked; and they sewed fig leaves together and made themselves coverings." Genesis 3:1-7 (NKJV)

So, we learn from this that Adam and Eve were created without sin, without the knowledge of good and evil. Satan mixed lies and truth together. When they ate of the fruit and disobeyed God, their eyes were opened to good and evil. This was the sin that caused death and the separation from God. How many times have I been deceived by Satan using lies and truth mixed together;

Have you? I can remember hearing him whispering "Go ahead! It will be fun! What can it hurt?" How about you? Have you ever heard and I don't mean audibly, but that little voice inside... I have heard it said that sin is fun for a season, but there are four seasons. It may be fun for one, but you pay the price in the other three. God is Holy and just and will not allow sin to go unpunished. And yet He knew we would sin, be separated from Him, and would need a pathway to be able to gain that relationship once again.

Ok, if evolution is the correct theory and we are an amazing cosmic "accident" then we have evolved over, (let's make up a really big number here that we can't really comprehend so we will just accept it as fact) gazillions of years into a miraculous being. I mean the mere idea that somehow some primordial goo's constituents accidentally bumped together and began to form life that is so amazingly complex that we STILL don't understand it boggles my "evolved" mind. And can this make sense unless evolution is a god we accept by faith and worship because it has created an amazing world in which we exist? Just consider the indisputable design of the human body, forget all the animals and plants etc. seriously? Chance, accident, coincidence? Just the ability that evolution has to repair and replace certain aspects of the process of life is astounding.

Truly we don't give the evolution god it's due. Now I admit I am sounding a bit sarcastic here but let's be honest. Haven't we elevated the theory of evolution to a religion? Isn't it a faith based conglomeration of theories that people adhere to. The dictionary defines religion as: 1) A set of beliefs concerning the cause, nature, and purpose of the universe, especially when considered as the creation of a superhuman agency or agencies, usually involving devotional and ritual observances, and often containing a moral code governing the conduct of human affairs. 2) A specific fundamental set of beliefs and practices generally agreed upon by a number of persons or sects; *the Christian religion; the Buddhist religion.*(dictionary.com) Faith is defined as: 1) confidence or trust in a person or thing. (dictionary.com) So over time we have replaced the term "theory of evolution" with just "evolution" and are expected it to be factual not theoretical. We are to discount the fact that macro evolution has never been proven as fact but is still theory, a theory demanding faith and therefore should be considered a religion. But the sad fact is, it won't because mankind wants a way to excuse his behavior and shirk responsibility for his actions.

Evolution offers no hope or purpose for our existence and yet it is embraced as the most sensible and logical reason for why we are here. But the logic is flawed no matter how many incomprehensible numbers of years is attached to it. What I mean is that the normal person, including me, has a difficult time comprehending the amount of time a million years is, much less a billion. And there is a reason for that. The reason is that it is easier to get us to believe it if we can't truly understand it. But the holes in the theory are just too big to ignore.

For instance, why are there two sexes that are dependent upon each other for procreation? I mean wouldn't it make sense that since evolution is so smart and calculating that we should be asexual with the ability to procreate individually. And then there is the question about death. Why do we die, in fact why does anything die? It seems logical that evolution is an amazing designer so why did it incorporate death or even disease into the mix for that matter? Now don't try to argue that disease evolved also because that would make no sense. If all life came from the primordial goo and miraculously transformed into life, a single celled organism that began evolving into every kind of life today, why would it ever decide to evolve into disease much less death?

Yeah, I know, you are arguing with me right now, quite possibly out loud asking me "how can you be so stupid? Don't you know that disease and death wasn't a part of evolutions plan it was just a byproduct of living in the world that has bacteria in it and that is what causes the disease and death." And I would say, "nice try" but the truth is that evolution makes no sense without it somehow having a controlling mechanism, or a "brain" so to speak. I mean there has to be something making the decisions for the next "phase" of evolution to occur. Consider the innumerable plants and animals on planet earth. Consider the humanity. Why all the variety? Why so many different species? Why doesn't every human being look alike? Or plants or animals for that matter? There are too many examples of the theory of evolution not working with actual provable science. For example, the human eye. There are several parts of the eye that had to have been formed simultaneously in order for the eye to work. Evolution supposedly doesn't work that way. As things are developing during evolution if something is of no value or deemed unnecessary then it is cast off for something better to replace it. For God's sake, I feel like an idiot simply trying to discuss this theory of evolution in a rational manner! Like I stated earlier, it simply makes no sense at all without a controlling element that makes decisions concerning the process. And that doesn't work with what we have been taught about evolution.

So, what does this have to do with you? One of the main theories attributed to evolution is the term "survival of the fittest".

129

Is this really the dominating characteristic that we want to reduce to this wonderful gift called life? Simply surviving? Now that may be a rational explanation for the animal kingdom however, let's reasonably look at our situation as human beings on planet earth. If you believe in evolution then you really have no reason to believe in anything beyond the here and now. Everything that we experience truly has no lasting purpose because everything has just happened purely by accident. We are here simply to survive, and for what? There is no design, no plan, no hope. Evolution is a topic that is argued by the educated and the uneducated. We all get to choose whether or not we buy into that belief system. Although it seems that there is a more concerted effort by governments and scientific entities that seek to proclaim this theory as actual fact, which it is not. I don't want to get into a debate about creation versus evolution, there are many more intelligent people and resources for you to study if you choose to do so. For the purposes of this book I want us to stay simple, logical, rational, and yet we still have to choose to believe in one or the other.

My family and I were recently in Washington DC as we were on our two-year travel around this wonderfully amazing country of ours. During our time there, we spent many days enjoying the great museums one of them being the Natural History Museum. They had a huge, very well-done display of the evolution of man with the different types of man that supposedly evolved from the primates. So many items were presented as factually correct when they have never been proven. And yet there we were, in a crowded room of people making the "ooooh's and Ahhhh's" of amazement of how far we have come or "evolved" over the gazillion years of evolution. It saddened me that there were so many school aged children there also being indoctrinated into this false belief. I simply said to myself and sometimes just a little louder to see if anyone was listening, "I wonder why there are still primates around if we evolved from them?" I said it loud enough to catch the ear of a few people who looked back at me like a dog does when they hear some unusual sound. You know the look, head cocked to one side and wide eyed. However, that was only momentary as the need to "ooooh" and "ahhhh" about the religion of evolution overtook them once again.

The point I am making here is that you have to believe something. You have to place your faith in something, some form of belief. You can't avoid it because you simply can't live your life without placing faith in something. That something can be in yourself which is a good thing to do from the standpoint of achieving goals and being successful in any given venture. And yet that pesky question still comes to mind…what about death? Again, my purpose is not to offend you, however, I am certain that there are many aspects of what I say here in this book is sure to offend and I am willing to take that chance. And if what I am presenting to you is not true but simply my belief that seems to have no merit then you haven't really given up anything but your time reading this. However, I believe it is worth offending because if what I am saying here IS true then I would rather offend you so that you would make the choice for life, eternal life with the God who created you with the desire that you would choose Him and the Eternal life that He offers. And not just life after death but abundant life here and now that offers peace, hope and purpose filled loving guidance from the God that created you, chose you, loves you and desires for you to love Him and choose Him back. Jesus said:

"The thief does not come except to steal, and to kill, and to destroy. I have come that they may have life, and that they may have it more abundantly" John 10:10 (NKJV)

"The Lord is not slack concerning His promise, as some count slackness, but is longsuffering toward us, not willing that any should perish but that all should come to repentance." 2Peter 3:9 (NKJV)

And remember that the Bible tells us that there is a Hell but it was not created for man, it was created as punishment for Satan and his angels that chose sin and to rebel and reject God. This is also the place where sin will be punished and destroyed, therefore if your sin is not forgiven by placing your faith and trust in Jesus this is your ultimate destination.

God loves us more than we can fathom. He wants us to know Him back, have a personal relationship with Him. Regardless of what you have heard or been taught He is real. You aren't an evolved ape over millions of years. That is one of those lies that Satan loves for people to believe. One of the lies Satan has been telling since the beginning of time; one of MANY. The thought concept of evolution incorporated with reincarnation has been around since ancient times however, the modern-day theory came about in the mid eighteenth century when Charles Darwin wrote, "On the Origin of Species". This began the snowball effect that has influenced millions worldwide. And don't you for one minute believe that this was by accident. Satan by his cunning is the master of deceiving millions into buying into this "theory". And many do so because they would rather believe this lie than to accept the truth that there is a God and they will answer to Him if not now, then one day.

You see, if we believe that we are evolved, then there is no God and we are just some cosmic accident. When this life is over there is nothing. We have nothing beyond this life to look forward to. And if this is correct then placing your faith in Jesus is simply a waste of time. However, if what I have been telling you is the truth the choice you make regarding Jesus will have eternal consequences; perhaps unintended but nonetheless eternal. Amazingly the theory is full of so many holes it truly astounds me that so many buy into it. Remarkably, some Christians take the path to least resistance and embrace evolution as part of God's plan. And now you ask yourself, "I read about it in a school book, I have been taught this in school and elsewhere since I was a child. How can it not be true?" And I answer you in telling you that it is a lie that has been told millions of times to millions of people.

Joseph Goebbels, an Adolph Hitler propagandist, is credited with saying this, "If you tell a big enough lie and keep repeating it people will eventually come to believe it. The Lie can be maintained only for such time as the State can shield the people from the political, economic and/or military consequences of the lie. It thus becomes vitally important for the State to use all of its powers to repress dissent, for the truth is the mortal enemy of the lie, and thus by extension, the truth is the greatest enemy of the State" (jewishvirtuallibrary.org) I believe you are aware of that name and this man's connection to the Holocaust and the Second World War.

Satan desires to destroy, deceive, and make us doubt. And he does so because when you believe that you are just an "accident" of nature then you have no hope. You have no purpose. After all you are just here for a short period of time and then you are gone, that's it. So ,what purpose could there be in life? It always amazes me that people who don't believe in God, who put their faith in evolution, still want to make some sort of impact with their lives. Why? If this is all there is and we weren't created for a purpose, and there is no God, then help me understand what joy you can truly experience in this thing called life? The answer is simple. Evolution is a lie. We were created by God who loves us and He has given us the choice to love Him back.

Pure and undefiled religion before God and the Father is this; to visit orphans and widows in their trouble, and to keep oneself unspotted from the world. James 1:27

12 Religions

Pride is one of the main reasons we don't pursue a relationship with God. Be honest, we all want to rule our own little kingdom called life. It's MY life, and I will live it as I please. My, me, mine… what's in it for me? What do I get out of it? If we relax our pride and humbly recognize that we have a need for forgiveness, we admit we have a NEED! No man is an island. So we come to the question of how to know God. There are religions that tell you that is impossible. He is too great a being to be known by our finite brains. Now hold on a minute and think about that. God made us, so in all reasonable, logical thinking, we have to believe that He wanted us. And for what purpose? Did He make us puppets or did He give us free will? He gave us choice so it stands to reason that He wants us to know Him. He made us and He is God so He knows us better than we know ourselves. Rick Warren made the wonderful point of fact in His book "The Purpose Driven Life," We cannot disappoint God. He already knows everything we are going to do. And in spite of all of that He still created us. So WHY? I am telling you that He wanted us and loves us and wanted a chosen relationship with us. He wanted us to choose Him back, love Him back. Logical reasoning is what we must use regardless of what we grew up in, or what we were taught. I came from a Christian home and I recognize that Jesus is the Truth not because I was taught that but because I have learned it through knowing God personally. I wish the same for you.

I cannot for the life of me reason why people believe the way that they do. I try to take into account environment, life experiences, culture etc. and that does give me reason for hope, however, when it comes to people born and raised in the United States of America, I am dumbfounded. Although reasonably I should not be, in fact it may come across as arrogant to think that the United States is in fact "United" when it comes to belief systems be they religious, political etc. Regardless of what anyone says, this country is diverse, and I mean diverse as in you can virtually find any likeminded opinion you choose. Don't believe me? Try traveling it and you will see. Of course, the old saying, "birds of a feather flock together" certainly rings true. Look at the regions of this country. Southern; Conservative Bible Belt, Northern; Liberal progressive, Midwest: little bit of both, West: little bit of conservative, majority liberal progressive AND ALL with psychological disorders abounding. The sad thing about Religions, although many are well intentioned, is that they are man-made. They are an idea about God, but not the truth about THE God. Ok but wait a minute. Didn't I just say that I came to know God through Religion? No, I said I came to know ABOUT God. There is a difference. I came to know God through faith IN Him.

What is it about God that makes people so afraid of Him? I mean I understand what the Bible says;

"The fear of the LORD is the beginning of wisdom;

A good understanding have all those who do His commandments.

His praise endures forever." Psalm 111:10 (NKJV)

The word "fear" in the Hebrew "yir'ah" also means respect, reverence. Perhaps we allow the "terror" aspect too much weight. Respect for something and fear of it makes sense. Lightning is something to be afraid of because it can kill you, so have respect for it. Don't go swimming in a thunderstorm. I think that we fear something we don't know. Maybe the reason people are so hesitant to know God is because they are afraid of Him, and rightly so, I mean we are sinful human beings. And when we are guilt ridden and feel unworthy, we certainly don't want to risk rejection or condemnation. Because of these feelings we may think we're out of luck. There are literally thousands of religions in the world today and each one proclaims that it is the "right" one, even when the religion espouses that there are many pathways to God. And this within itself is confusing because if there are many pathways to God and they contradict each other on so many levels how can they be true? SO, I present to you this observation that I have stated so many times before; religion is man-made, relationship is God made. In other words, mankind continues to invent ways to reach God through rules and regulations, through hierarchy and position. But God, from the beginning has simply wanted for us to have a relationship with Him. In fact, it was the reason that He created us.

I am not claiming to be an expert in theology but I am an expert in my relationship to God. And as a result, I have found myself so disturbed, angered, and mostly saddened by the misrepresentations of God. The longer I have known God and all of the amazing ways that He has taught me about Himself should make those emotions understandable to you. After all, if you had a close, lifelong friend that you knew people were telling lies about, or misrepresenting their character or simply making up things that weren't true about them, would you not feel the same? And therefore, my desire to share what I know about Him in this little book. And the most important aspect I wish for you to take away from this information that I give to you is that this is all about you. It is your choice as to what you believe. I want you to know The God that I know. Once again, not a god, or god as who I imagine that he is but THE GOD. And the most amazing thing about that is that you will have your own unique relationship with Him, and yet it will be very similar. You see The God is unchanging. He is who He is and will always be who He is. His love will never fail and His desire for you to choose to love Him back will never end. And knowing God is possible because of the Gospel of Jesus Christ that is also unchanging. Gospel, now there is a word that many are familiar with and yet many are not so I will expand upon it. The term Gospel holds a lot of meanings probably the most important one is that it is the "Good News". dictionary.com gives several definitions but I will list two; 1) the teachings of Jesus and the apostles; the Christian revelation. 2) glad tidings, especially concerning salvation and the kingdom as announced to the world by Jesus the Christ.

You see, to someone who is confused or wondering about why we are here, if we were created then Who created us, Why hasn't this creator given us some kind of information about themselves etc. , and How do we get to know this creator, then discovering the answers to these questions is GOOD NEWS! So, I am honored that you would give me the opportunity, better yet, the blessing of sharing this Good News with you. It's understandable that you may not agree with everything that I share. You may come from a different world view than I do or a different religious background. That excites me that you are willing to challenge what you believe. I certainly have over the course of my life and have never discovered any man-made religion to stand up against knowing the God and what He did in order for me to come to know Him. Every other religion that I studied always came with requirements that I had to meet in order for me to be worthy of its system of religion. And that is why you will see this over and over again in this book. Religion is man-made, Relationship is God made.

"Now wait just a minute," I can hear you say, "you are promoting a religion and isn't it also man made?" That is a very good question and a fine point that I will try to explain here but will hopefully be better answered as we go along. Judaism and Christianity are an intertwined religion although there are many Jewish people who will disagree with this statement. However, I am talking to you about someone who knows the Jewish people rather well considering He created them and established these people as the "chosen people" through whom He "chose" to show the world who He is. Let's take the first definition of religion; 1) a set of beliefs concerning the cause, nature, and purpose of the universe, especially when considered as the creation of a superhuman agency or agencies, usually involving devotional and ritual observances and other containing a moral code governing the conduct of human affairs.(dictionary.com) Yep that is a long definition but necessary. It is necessary to recognize Judaism and Christianity as religions. God in His infinite wisdom certainly knew that mankind would invent a whole lot of religions over the course of its history. Even though Adam and Eve knew God personally and shared their history with Him with their descendants, as time went on this knowledge was corrupted and misrepresented. Most of this was oral tradition until writing was developed as a way of communicating.

There are so many religions in the world today. So many people wonder which one to believe. Perhaps if we just live the majority of our lives with high moral values then when all is said and done at its end, we will tilt the scales in our favor, having done more good things than bad. Well, that's all nice and good…for Hollywood, but with God it doesn't work. The Bible says that there is none righteous, not a single solitary soul. In fact, it says that our best efforts are as filthy rags to God. In other words, there is nothing that we can do to deserve the Heaven He has created for us. But He loves us and made a way through Jesus. Our job is to believe it and trust Him with our lives, more importantly, have the intimate relationship with us that He desires for us to have.

Throughout the centuries, mankind has invented various religions to offer hope to its followers. Many of these religions offer more to do with control than freedom. Freedom to hope. God wants a relationship with us. Yes, God wants. Amazing isn't it? God wanting; I mean think about that, He is God and He wants. You would think that anything He wants He could have with simply thinking it. Really, He is the creator of the universe, all knowing, all powerful so why does He still want?

Aha! That's where Jesus comes in! That is one of the reasons it was imperative that God became flesh and dwelt among us! Jesus showed no rejection or condemnation. Except to the pharisees who pretended to know God but didn't.

Hope. What is life without hope? We wish for things, good health, wealth, friends, etc. and we do what we can to ensure that we achieve these things. But there are so many things over which we have no control. So, we hope. Religion gives hope. But there is a problem with religion. Religion is man-made. Relationship is God made.

The purpose of this discussion is religions. Having recently watched the series hosted by Morgan Freeman about God, I was amazed at how every belief system that he presents to the audience includes a belief in a Deity and was embraced as good and acceptable. Well, I guess it has to be for some, especially the producers who are trying to please everyone and want the show to be a success. Mr. Freeman did an excellent job of hiding his opinion if it was negative, the sign of a seasoned host. Although there were times that his expressions were not edited out and clearly showed a wide-eyed amazement. Now whether that was a "wow" amazement, or a "you've got to be kidding me" amazement is left to your interpretation. Every time I look at Mr. Freeman all I can think of is the character he portrayed in Shawshank Redemption named "Red". A truly likable and wise person that is a survivor and extremely capable man who eventually learned the importance of hope.

So, my frustration with the religions around the world is that they seem so unreasonable. Now mind you, I was raised in the Conservative Bible Belt South and became what is known as a "Christian" when I was nine years old. And I guess to many my "religion" may seem unreasonable also. But there is one aspect to being a Christian that I find appealing and that is that God has done the work. He has made it possible to know Him by believing in Jesus and what He did for us. I don't have to earn it, or qualify for it, I simply have to believe it, and it begins my relationship with Him and gives me the ability to live my life the way He wants it to be. Because He knows what is best for me. A relationship with Jesus it is based upon discovering the truth; not "my" truth, or "your" truth but THE TRUTH. And he is THE TRUTH. Doesn't it make reasonable sense that IF there is a God, He created us, and He gave us this amazing world in which to live, He wouldn't want us running around like chickens with their heads cut off? Sorry, Southern kicking in, doesn't it make sense that God must be smart enough to want us to know THE truth, especially when it comes to Him?

I live in the United States of America. Some have said that in my country there is no way that people have not heard about Jesus, but I am finding that to be false. What I have discovered is that so many people reject Christianity because it is considered an organized religion that is mainly concerned with getting money and controlling people. Many believe that It is simply one of thousands of religions throughout the world that is full of fairy tales and nice stories but really is just one of many. I can understand how this is so. Christianity is a religion that describes those who choose to follow Jesus Christ and His teachings. These people believe that Jesus is the Son of God as He claimed to be. Because of this claim, He was branded a heretic and subsequently put to death. He claimed that He would rise again from the grave proving that He was who He claimed to be. Christians believe this to be true. The Bible gives us evidence of the fact that Jesus rose from the grave. A man, beaten almost to death with His skin barely hanging onto His body, nailed hands and feet to a cross, lifted into the air so that the slow agony of suffocation insured death, was pierced through His side was most assuredly dead. He had hung on the cross for six hours. They buried Him in a tomb and three days later, just as He had said, He physically arose from the grave having defeated death and proving that He was indeed God in the flesh. He was seen by over 500 people after His resurrection. He spent forty days on earth with His disciples preparing them for what lay ahead of them in their lives. And I might add that every one of these disciples except one, died a martyr's death. Some of them horribly gruesome torturous death and yet none of them denied that Christ was who He said He was. In fact, they were killed for preaching that Jesus was God in the flesh, God the Son who came to earth, died for our sins and rose from the grave and is alive and in Heaven even as I write these words. So, I ask you to use your rational, logical, reasonable mind and explain why these men would willingly give their lives for a lie? Why would people alive today be willing to give their lives for a lie? I tell you that they didn't because what they gave their lives for is the truth. Jesus is the only way to know God the Father and God the Holy Spirit.

The simplicity of God is Jesus, believing He is who He said He was. Also understand that although it may sound arrogant to say so but the truth is that He is the ONLY way. And those are not my words but His;

"Jesus said to him, "I am the way, the truth, and the life. No one comes to the Father except through Me." John 14:6 (NKJV)

The fact that Jesus was a man who lived approximately two thousand years ago in the area now known as Israel is not reasonably disputed. There are historical documents that are not religious that give credence to this fact. Who He was and is are what many people seem to have a problem with.

If all the other religions all lead to God, believing that God loves diversity and variety then why wouldn't God like variety in religion? You can make a rational argument that this must be true because of all the different religions out there who claim to seek God. And there truly are very many good- hearted people who seek THE GOD but are deceived due to their belief in a man-made way to do this. There is not more diversity in any religion more than there is in the body of Christ, also known as, the Church. Born-Again believers in Jesus come from every walk of life, every tribe and nation and this religion transcends every culture and background of humanity because of the truth of what it is. It is the only basis for a true relationship with the one and true living, all powerful, all knowing, loving God. And the supernatural occurrence that is a part of becoming a child of God by being born again and the filling of the Holy Spirit testifies to this. The reason being that this is the truth of God. The message of God's love for mankind and His provision of forgiveness and reconnection with mankind through the sacrifice of Christ Jesus rings true to the heart of man which is forever searching for something to fill this God shaped hole. (don't forget that God said have no other Gods before me as a warning for this, already at that time there were multitudes of false gods that were worshipped, pagan gods). Hopefully you are familiar with the story of Moses in the Bible. If not, you can read about it in the book of Exodus. There was a time when Moses was dealing with Pharaoh desiring to get the freedom of the Israelite nation, the plagues etc., then they were in the wilderness where God gave them the Ten Commandments. This is because God's desire and plan was to show the world who He is through these "chosen people". This is why the world has sought to destroy the Jews for so long. It is directly as a result of Satan's hatred for the truth of who God really is and that he is not God and desires to be. He will do everything in his power to deceive. Look at the world today. Has not Israel been a focus of hatred in the middle east?

However, even within the Christian religion there are denominations that are corrupted due to man's influence rather than God's. The different theologies, rules and regulations, you have to dress this way, ladies you can't wear makeup, men you must wear a coat and tie, you have to preach from the King James Bible, you can't have instrumental music in the church, etc. etc. etc.… It's all a distraction from simply getting together with fellow born again believers and encouraging each other, learning from and most importantly loving each other. And the truth is that every denomination probably has a few things wrong that aren't exactly as God would have them to be, however, having the main understanding of the need to repent or turn away from sin, and become a born again believer in Jesus is the one uniting aspect in spite of all of the idiosyncrasies within the denominations.

BUT YOU MUST UNDERSTAND THIS; my anger is not against the good-hearted people who follow these religions with good intentions. My anger is the actions that those without good intentions have perpetrated to obtain and maintain power. This is Satanic from the start. Remember that iniquity was found in Satan because of his pride and covetous attitude towards God. He wanted the power, the ultimate power. When I talk against religion it is because I am angry at those who have used a religion to gain power over people whose desire it is to know God. And they have been lied to. The only way to have a personal relationship with God is through Jesus His Son. If you are a Christian and reading this then I ask you; "Do you have a personal relationship with God?" You must be honest here, you can't depend on what you have achieved yourself such as baptism, catechism, attending church services, Mass, etc. all of those are rules and tenets designed to keep you dependent on the law of following rules, not the grace of God given when you place your faith in Jesus Christ. If you are of a religion that teaches that you cannot know God personally don't you see the absurdity in that teaching? That is such a lie! Why would God create you and not give you everything you need to know Him? No, religion is all about power also. Keeping you in line, following a strict set of rules, requirements that have to be met in order to be a part of the religion, or whatever leader that can dictate over you. This is not God's plan at all. Use your God given logical mind!

And although Christianity is certainly designated as a religion, the focus of it is the relationship with God. He has made it possible for us to have a relationship with us so that we may live our lives with Him as Lord collaborating with us in our lives. He wishes to direct us not dictate to us. He wants us to choose to obey Him and His direction for our lives because He is THE God and knows what is best for us. But understand this, all other religions have requirements that YOU must achieve in order to earn your position with God or be deserving of His favor and obtain entry into whatever idea of an afterlife they espouse. Every religion, every belief system other than Christianity is a distraction from the truth.

There is a battle for the souls of the apples of God's eye, humanity, and it is a battle with Satan, a spiritual battle that is growing in intensity every day and I will discuss this more in the next chapter. More people are alive on the planet than have ever been before. The foundations were set so many years ago. God is a sovereign God and His plan, will ultimately be fulfilled, He has already defeated Satan at the cross by the sacrificial death of Jesus. The price for our sins required by a righteous God has been paid by the blood of Jesus. There is no other religion where the God willingly gives of Himself so that mankind can be saved and live an eternity with Him. All other religions demand that you somehow earn this ability. THE God offers mankind the free gift of eternal life by simply turning away from sin, accepting by faith in what Jesus did through His sinless life, death, and most importantly His resurrection from the dead showing that He is God the Son with the power over sin and death. This is true Christianity.

Being a Christian should mean a follower, or believer in Jesus the Christ, or as many say, "Jesus Christ". The Christ part comes from the Greek meaning "Messiah". So, when someone says they are a Christian they should mean that they believe in Jesus as the Messiah or "Christ". However, don't be confused, all of these false religions, all of the misrepresentations of true Christianity, none of this was a surprise to God, in fact the amazing aspect of God and His sovereignty is His ability to adjust His plan according to what He knows we are going to do. He knew that all of these false religions would be established and followed literally by billions of people. He also knew and planned that His word and His truth about the redemption through Jesus would also be made available during this time. Furthermore, it was His plan to provide mankind with the miracle of the Holy Spirit being poured out to mankind after Jesus returned to Heaven. And it is by the indwelling of the Holy Spirit as a result of being Born Again that we have the relationship to God. He comes to live in us, we become His temple!

"Do you not know that you are the temple of God and that the Spirit of God dwells in you?" 1 Corinthians 3:16 (NKJV)

Sadly, there are even those who are Born Again Believers in Jesus who continue to live as babies in their faith, never growing and developing their immediate connection to God made possible only by the sacrifice of Jesus. Being tuned out of the Holy Spirit connection by being so caught up in distractions of life is like trying to hold sand, it continues to run through our fingers and although you desire to possess it, it eludes your control. But God is a solid rock upon which we may tightly hold on to and He will not fall from our hands and will not allow us to fall from His!

"My sheep hear my voice, and I know them, and they follow me. And I give them eternal life, and they shall never perish; neither shall anyone snatch them out of my hand. My Father, who has given them to me, is greater than all; and no one is able to snatch them out of my Father's hand. I AND MY FATHER ARE ONE." John 10:27-30 (NKJV)

When we consider our idea of God instead of try to understand who He truly is we are simply wasting our time. Imagining God to be who you think He should be is an arrogant fool's errand and can be dangerous. There are 7 plus billion people on this planet, imagine if each one of them decides how they imagine God is and acts accordingly. Well, actually that to some degree is what is happening in the world even as I type this. Everyone cannot be right in imagining who and what God is. There are so many conflicting views in the world of religions today. Reincarnation, polytheism, animal worship, planet worship, you name it and there probably is some religion that adheres to some sort of worship of a deity that relates.

If it is possible for God to feel frustration then I am quite sure he certainly does when it comes to our speculation of who He is in relation to who He actually is. I mean let's think of this for a minute. Here is God all knowing, all powerful, everywhere, and yet He cannot get humanity on the same page regarding who He is. God is perfect, He can't make a plan that will fail, He can't learn something, He can't be surprised, He can't be disappointed, He can't be wrong. But He is God and we are not so it's hard to relate to how He designed a plan that would get the information about who He is to us knowing full well of our capability to absolutely screw the whole system up. Now as a Christian or once again I will say Born Again believer in Jesus Christ, I am fully aware that the Bible is in fact the message system that He supernaturally designed for mankind to understand who and what He is. But we as "know it all" human beings are so arrogant that we believe there has to be some other way to know God. We make up who we believe God to be and that is why I continue to say religion is man-made relationship is God made. And in all of our haughty conceit and self-worship we continue to design the God we desire rather than discover the God who is. This is why the Bible is so important in understanding that there is but one God and the only way to know about Him is through the Bible which is also considered to be His word.

It's the reason He took thousands of years using multiple people, actually over 40 different authors of the books in the old and New Testament's, so that no one could say that this was contrived and planned by man. But the most important aspect of the Bible that separates this holy book from all other religious holy books is that it contains prophecy. Prophecy can be considered to be pre-written history. Now this may sound peculiar to someone because how can you pre-write history? Well, if you were God and are outside of time, you can see any particular part of that time. For us who are in time things that have passed are considered history, because they have already happened. When God looks at mankind, he sees time as one complete unit which contains past present and future according to us but to him it is all happening at once. Thus, the name he gave to Moses for himself, I AM. So, in His word, the Bible, He has given us prophecy, or pre written history of what is going to happen in our future proving that He is not a god, but the God.

Understand this, that when these books were written some thousands of years ago, the language of that day and the description of things that are present hundreds of years later are understandably challenging to understand. And yet the most important parts are not written this way. For example:

"For God so loved the world that he gave his only begotten Son, that whoever believes in Him should not perish but have everlasting life." John 3:16 (NKJV)

This is the most famous verse of the entire Bible and rightfully so. But when you start reading prophecies in the book of Daniel, or Ezekiel, or the book of Revelation, you understandably may become confused by symbolism or descriptions that may have made better sense in the day of the author and yet are somewhat confusing today. But God had a purpose in doing this because the Bible being God's word is not simply a literary achievement. It's not simply a Book full of fairytales and nice stories. It is a book filled with purpose, history, consequences, wisdom, but most importantly warnings. You see prophecy is a way of letting us know what to prepare for. There were prophecies regarding Jesus as the Messiah. And not simply the conquering king Messiah but the suffering and dying Messiah. But for our purposes what is in the Bible about the times in which we are living and are quickly headed towards are vitally important. But if you are not a member of the family of God, you do not have the indwelling of the Holy Spirit of God you are at a great disadvantage when attempting to fully grasp what God is showing in his word. In fact, the Bible tells us that the gospel message, or "good news" that the Bible contains appears to be foolishness to those who are perishing.

"For the message of the cross is foolishness to those who are perishing, but to us who are being saved it is the power of God." 1 Corinthians 1:18 (NKJV)

And understand this, you are perishing if you are not a Born-Again believer in Jesus Christ.

Have you seen this before? Religion is man-made, relationship is God made. It is true that I came to know about God through religion, but I came to know God through my relationship to Him. If you don't have a relationship to God, you can't really know Him. You can look at all the pictures you want of the Grand

Canyon. There are some amazing photographs, movies etc. However, until you experience it live and in person, you cannot truly experience that feeling of awesome wonderment. You have to experience it first-hand. Same is with a Big Mac. Yes, I am a McDonalds fan, so don't hate. I can describe a Big Mac to you, two all-beef patties, special sauce, lettuce, cheese, pickles, onions, on a sesame seed bun. Sounds delish right? But until you actually taste one you can only imagine what it tastes like. You have to experience it to know it.

First let's remember that God is omnipotent and omniscient. Meaning He knows everything and is all powerful. SO, doesn't it make sense that He can get the message He desires to get to you at any time? Isn't it possible that He did choose say 40 or so men over thousands of years to write down things that He wanted you to know in your lifetime? Couldn't He have planned for all of these writings or "scripture" to be compiled and put into book form for the time when planet earth would have the most inhabitants it would ever have? Remember, the printing press was only invented in 1440 and the first King James Bible wasn't printed until 1611.

But there are so many religions out there so how do we know how to address THE God who is the creator? Since we acknowledge that our belief in God is based upon our faith in His existence, it makes logical sense that we should want to know that we are addressing THE God and not some pretender to His throne. And this is where the problem of all the manmade religions in the world come into the equation. Once again logic demands that all of these religions cannot be correct. They cannot all acknowledge and recognize, much less worship and respect THE one true God. The reason that I can reasonably say this is to pose this question; Why would God who most assuredly knows who and what He is be willing to accept multitudes of mischaracterizations of who and what HE IS? The answer is that He doesn't.

Remember, He is God, perfect and His ways and our ways are different. You can reasonably look at a number of religions today and recognize that the illogic of them being of the one true God is obvious. For example, why would God choose one man and suddenly give him and only him revelation regarding who He is and what He wants done? History is replete with men beginning cults claiming that they have had a revelation from God with something new that God "forgot" to do a while back so He decided to tell this person now because He forgot or He hadn't taken certain aspects of humanity into consideration etc. Do you get the absurdity of this yet? The perfect God who undoubtedly has a perfect plan all of a sudden, needs to give a revelation to an individual. I am speaking of religions such as Islam and Mormonism. Both of these religions began as a result of one man receiving a revelation from God. In other words, God apparently made a mistake. What is interesting about these two particular religions is that they both claim that they were needed because something was missing in the initial release of the Judeo-Christian religion. I don't buy into these things. I believe in the God of Abraham, Isaac, and Jacob, also known as Judaism which is completed, perfectly I might add, through Jesus Christ, and thus the religion known as Christianity. The Religions of Judaism and Christianity are truly one complete relationship device from God that mankind has given the designation of Religion. Have I stated before that Religion is manmade and relationship is God made?

There is nothing easy about being a Christian. Becoming one is very simple, as simple as believing and receiving the gift God offers. But living the Christian life in this day and age is extremely challenging. As Born-Again Believers in Jesus we are called to exemplify his life, to love our enemies, take care of the "least of these," even lay down our lives for our brother. But if you go to most churches today, the example of Jesus is sometimes hard to find. Perhaps this is why the world is rejecting the organized religion of Christianity. Not the Gospel of Jesus Christ mind you but the "Organized Religion" we call Christianity.

Most of my life I have been a Southern Baptist and I am very thankful for the blessings this denomination has afforded me in my spiritual walk with Jesus. Having studied many of the Christian denominations and their practices or beliefs, I recognize that the Baptist faith tends to be the simplest and for lack of a better term, "childlike" denominations in the Religion of Christianity. What I mean is that it is basic and simple and easily understood, much like what I believe that Jesus taught and wanted us to hear and receive.

Jesus was and is the Son of God, the second person of the Trinity who became "became flesh and dwelt among us" (John 1:14 NKJV) He was born of the Virgin Mary, lived a sinless life, was crucified on a cross, died, was buried and three days later arose from the grave. He ascended to Heaven and is seated at the right hand of God the Father, the first person of the Trinity. He defeated sin and death in our place, and has promised to come back for us where we may be with Him forever. We are saved or "born again" by grace, not by works so that no one can claim that they "earned" their salvation.

We believe in and practice "emersion baptism" meaning that when you are baptized your entire body goes under the water signifying the death, burial, and resurrection of Jesus. We do this in obedience to the command of Christ who instructed His disciples to;

"Go therefore and make disciples of all the nations, baptizing them in the name of the Father and of the Son and of the Holy Spirit." Matthew 28:19 (NKJV)

And I might just add for those who don't recognize the Trinity as being something that is spoken of in the Bible, take note that these are Jesus' words and instructions.

Every Southern Baptist Church that I have been associated with has basically been autonomous. Meaning that they are self-governing as far as their staff is concerned. The church body forms a committee to search for a pastor, then they recommend a candidate and the church membership votes on whether or not to "call" or basically "hire" the candidate. If they are chosen the new pastor chooses their staff etc. that will administer the requirements of the church. As a church that is a member of the Southern Baptist Convention there are certain requirements that must also be met in order to maintain membership with like-minded churches. They have an annual convention and vote on directors of various aspects of the Convention as well as determine where they stand concerning spiritual matters that may be of concern on a national level. I won't go into further detail I think you get the point that I am trying to make.

Even though I consider the Christian Religious Denomination Southern Baptist to be the simplest, it is still more complicated than one would imagine. And I believe that this is by the infiltration of Satan's deception and work within the church. Don't be surprised that I suggested that Satan has influence in the church, actually it wasn't a suggestion rather a fact. Don't misunderstand me here, Satan is subtle and very cunning in his work. Remember when I stated earlier that every distraction that keeps us from a relationship with God is of Satan. Well, then don't be surprised when I tell you that Satan is alive and well and living and working in the church, also known as the Bride of Christ. And it is beyond time where we banished him and his influence or distraction from doing the work of Christ Jesus and focusing on making disciples instead of seat warmers.

There is a term called righteous indignation meaning morally right or justifiable and I am one of those people who can't seem to shut up when I see things that should be spoken about. This often irritates my wife but after 25 years of being married to me and knowing me for 32 years she just takes it in stride. I truly believe there are things for which we must take a stand when we know they are right, regardless of the "popular" opinion.

Although this is not exactly the best analogy it makes a good point. There is a story in the Gospel of Mark of a blind beggar named Bartimaeus who begins to shout at Jesus when He comes near and those around Him tell him basically to shut up which in turn causes Bartimaeus to shout even more loudly which gets Jesus' attention.

"Now they came to Jericho. As He went out of Jericho with His disciples and a great multitude, blind Bartimaeus, the son of Timaeus, sat by the road begging. And when he heard that it was

Jesus of Nazareth, he began to cry out and say, 'Jesus, Son of David, have mercy on me!'

Then many warned him to be quiet; but he cried out all the more, 'Son of David, have mercy on me!'

So Jesus stood still and commanded him to be called.

Then they called the blind man, saying to him, 'Be of good cheer. Rise, He is calling you.'

And throwing aside his garment, he rose and came to Jesus.

So Jesus answered and said to him, 'What do you want Me to do for you?'

The blind man said to Him, 'Rabboni, that I may receive my sight.'

Then Jesus said to him, 'Go your way; your faith has made you well.' And immediately he received his sight and followed Jesus on the road." Mark 10:46-52 (NKJV)

I have considered myself a Blind Bartimaeus several times in my walk with Jesus. The truth is that I was blinded or better yet distracted by things that appeared to be normal within our church but still recognized the need to bring them to someone's attention. Only to be silenced by those around me. And of what benefit is this you ask? Well, I will tell you that it is not always popular. Especially to the folk who like things the way they have "always been done" or with which they are comfortable. Churches are notorious in this regard. And I can say that in the Christian religion and all of its denominations, even non-denominational congregations, tend to have groups of like-minded people who are never satisfied with anything. They are the ones who can complain about anything. In the Baptist churches I have been involved with over the course of my life, and there have been quite a few, I have found this to be a sad truth. They find the absolute most childish things about which to argue and this causes dissension and doubt within the church body. Distractions seeded, watered, and grown by Satan himself.

Thankfully there are the faithful who don't allow themselves to get caught up in the politics of the church. They are the ones who are looking to serve and share their gifts with other members of the church and beyond. But understand this now and please get it into your head, you will never find a perfect church. And if you do, by all means don't join it because you will no doubt ruin their track record! Seriously, there is no such thing as a perfect church. There will always be some people that rub you the wrong way, or don't agree with certain things the way you do. But that's ok and to be expected because people are human beings with faults and insecurities etc. The most important aspect when looking for a church home is God's direction. First and foremost, you should seek His will for you and your family if that fits your description. Asking for God's direction for a church home is paramount which goes along with establishing your relationship with Him. Trusting that He will direct you to the right place of worship for you and your family is a part of growing in your relationship with Him. And never take Him out of the equation believing that you should be capable of doing something like that on your own.

When I was looking for a church home a short time after I had left and moved to another state to attend college, I attended a non-denominational service with a friend. The service was somewhat different to what I had been accustomed. A little more Pentecostal, meaning there was dancing and people speaking in tongues, or what I perceived to be that. I was a little uncomfortable but then I heard the Pastor preach a wonderful message full of the truth of God's word. I went up to him after the service and explained my position. How I loved the preaching but was a little confused by all the other "trappings" of the church members. He gave me a great analogy that I and my family use to this day. Finding a church home is kind of like looking for a regular home in which you plan to live. You search until you find the one that first of all has what you need. For example; if you need three bedrooms, don't settle for one with two. If you need two bathrooms don't settle for one. But let's say you find one that you really like, it has just the right number of bedrooms and bathrooms but the living room is just a bit too small. But that is something you can live with, right? The rest of the house just "feels" like home regardless of the one or two minor things that aren't perfect. And so it is with finding a place of worship, or church home. Everything won't be perfect, maybe not everything is what you are used to, but the Pastor is a God-fearing preacher of the Word of God without compromise and you find that there are ministries that you can plug into and give and receive in them.

So many people with which I have spoken about attending church, especially those who no longer attend any church on a regular basis, are usually the ones who are looking to see what they can get out of the experience. In my opinion this is one of the reasons that church attendance has steadily decreased over the recent years. People tend to look for a place that provides something for them and their family. Like does the church have a gym for the kids to play, or how many services do they have so we can choose the one that fits our schedule the best. Or do they have the right kind of music we like etc. And this is truly sad, and I can state that emphatically because I have been one of these people. I was looking for what I could get out of my experience instead of looking for where I could give and use the gifts God has given to me to edify the body. Don't get me wrong, the preaching/teaching of God's word is of utmost importance along with the fellowship with other Born-Again Believers but I, like so many good hearted, well intentioned people searched for a place where I felt like I could get my needs met. Somewhere over the course of the history of the church, we have been distracted into this way of thinking. And what should we do about it?

I firmly believe the answer is that we stop looking for what we can get and focus on what we can give. And I am not talking about financially although the most assuredly is a command to be followed. We, as the Bride of Christ should recognize the relationship that a Bride takes on in the marriage. God described Eve who would be the Bride of Adam as his "help meet" meaning that there were responsibilities that Eve would be suited for better than Adam in order to achieve God's plan for them. In other words, we must recognize that Jesus desires to work in us and through us through His Holy Spirit who has given EVERY Born-Again Believer at least one spiritual gift that is intended to edify the church body. Somewhere along the way we have lost the focus on these Spiritual Gifts. How did this happen?

My opinion is that in our human nature we have elevated some spiritual gifts to be more important than others which is the mark of Satan's influence. Paul taught the early church and thereby the church today that we should consider every spiritual gift of vital importance to the important working of the church as a whole. In fact, he was so disturbed at how many of the first century church were focusing on speaking in tongues as being extremely important, ever more so than other gifts. Paul chastised the early church about this using the analogy of our physical bodies and how could we assign more importance to one part over another. And that if one part of the body suffers, the entire body suffers. There is a great joke that goes along with this thought process:

All the parts of the body were having a meeting, trying to decide who was the one in charge…

"I should be in charge," said the brain, "because I run all the body's systems, so without me nothing would happen."

"I should be in charge," said the blood, "because I circulate oxygen all over so without me, you'd waste away."

"I should be in charge," said the stomach, "because I process food and give all of you, energy."

"I should be in charge," said the legs, "because I carry the body wherever it needs to go."

"I should be in charge," said the eyes, "because I allow the body to see where it goes."

"I should be in charge," said the rectum, "because I am responsible for waste removal."

All the other body parts laughed at the rectum and insulted him, so in a huff, he shut down tight. Within a few days, the brain had a terrible headache, the stomach was bloated, the legs got wobbly, the eyes got watery, and the blood was toxic. They all decided that the rectum should be the boss.

The moral of the story is that often times the person who is given the least amount of importance may in fact be one if not the most important person at any given time.

Perhaps it is vitally important that we view all parts of the Bride of Christ or the Church Body as equally important but most important is the work we do as the earthly "help meet" of our Groom, Our Lord and Savior Jesus Christ. But if we fail to recognize our gift or gifts given to us by the Holy Spirit for the edification of the church, how can we be using them and benefiting the believers in the command given by Jesus for us to make disciples? Remember, Jesus didn't just say to go out into the world and get people saved, He commanded us to make disciples and there is a difference. Please don't misunderstand me in this. Evangelism is so important and is also listed by Paul as a gift given by the Holy Spirit. And bringing people to the knowledge of the Good News of Jesus is the beginning of discipleship, but let's not elevate any gift above another because we need to understand the unity that should be focused upon that Jesus emphasized when He asked the Father to make us one just as He is one with the Father.

"Now I am no longer in the world but these are in the world, and I come to you. Holy Father, keep through Your name those who You have given Me, that they may be one as We are." John 17:11(NKJV)

"I do not pray for these alone, but also for those who will believe in Me through their word: that they may be one, as You, Father , are in Me, and I in You; that they also may be one in Us, that the world may believe that You sent Me." John 17:20-21 (NKJV)

In other words, Jesus wants His Bride to function as one unit doing the will of the Father just as He did as He walked the earth during His earthly ministry. And in order to do so, we must each be aware of the gift or gifts the Holy Spirit has bestowed upon us in order to do the best with what we have. And this is done in order to bring Glory to God the Father and Jesus Christ the Son.

Now there is a word that is so often misused and misunderstood in the body; Glory. I will freely admit that I am one of those people who used that word many times, sang it in hymns and praise songs, shouted, "Glory to God" and just simply believed that it was a term that was just a form of praise. I didn't learn until much later in my walk with the Lord as to the significance of the word. To bring God Glory is to in effect act as a mirror to His majesty, His likeness, reflecting the essence of who He is. So often I have asked other's during the course of my writing this little book what their opinion of the reason for life. Many Born Again Believers freely answered, "to bring God Glory." And I of course would ask them what they meant by that. Most would describe it as bringing God praise, or giving Him praise. In other words, they believed that the purpose of our existence or creation is to bring God continual praise. And that sounds all well and good until you ponder it for a while and try to understand that. Seriously, do we believe that God created us to simply give Him praise? That our existence on this planet along with all that life itself entails, that the end result is to be ever existing praise to God for eternity?

Don't get me wrong, I believe God deserves our praise and certainly desires for us to praise Him but the truest praise we can give to God the Father is to become more like His Son Jesus the Christ and reflect the essence of who He is back. And that essence of God is most assuredly Love. So, our most effective way of glorifying God is to love in the most perfect way as Jesus did. And this begins with loving Him with all of our heart, soul, mind, and strength and to let that love radiate to others. And that radiation comes as a result of us knowing God personally, deeply, with a desire to know Him more and more. Now having said all of that, do you know what your Spiritual Gift(s) are? Are you using them to edify the body of Christ? If not, why? Perhaps you have never been taught the importance of the spiritual gifts! Let me tell you how I discovered mine.

I became a Born-Again Believer in Jesus when I was nine years old. I began my walk with Him as a child with the childlike faith expected of a nine-year old. I loved going to church to learn more about Jesus and the work He accomplished while He walked this earth. And yet I often would find myself questioning some of the things I was taught. Not as to whether they were true or not but was that all there was to the story. So many times, I felt as if there was always something more that could be learned but being a young man, I simply accepted the basics and tried to satisfy myself with that. I remember learning the scripture in James that taught;

"If any of you lacks wisdom, let him ask of God, who gives to all liberally and without reproach, and it will be given to him." James 1:5 (NKJV)

I knew that Solomon was considered the wisest person in the Bible and it was because He asked God for that wisdom when given the opportunity to have many other things many common men would have settled for. So, I decided that I wanted to be wise also. But remember, as I discovered in my youthful indiscretions, that just because you may have wisdom doesn't mean that you always will use it.

In my teenage years I grew in my relationship to Jesus as a result of the wonderful youth group at our church and the many adults who lovingly taught us there. I began many wonderful friendships there and many who have continued on throughout my life. It was during these teenage years that I found myself being the person a lot of my friends would seek for advice regarding various things they were facing in their lives. And many times, I was amazed at myself for giving what I thought was very wise advice, and without fail always accompanied by scripture to back up that advice. Many times, I nearly broke my arm attempting to pat myself on the back because I thought that I was an amazing young man with the wisdom of Solomon. Man oh man, youthful arrogance run amok. It wasn't until years later when I was questioned by someone as to what my spiritual gift was. And like so many even today, I did not have a good response so I made it my goal to discover what my spiritual gift is.

So, I took a few "Spiritual gifts" inventory tests. If you are not familiar with what these are let me suggest you google search for one, or several if you are like me and want to know without a doubt. They basically ask you questions regarding your likes and dislikes, desires, aspects of your spiritual walk that you may find more interesting than others. Also, they ask questions such as have you ever found yourself being able to do something that you didn't know you had the ability to do, and in my case, it was to give good spiritual, bible-based advice. I discovered that I had been given the gift of exhortation which basically gives the ability to draw discernment and understanding from scripture which is not common to everyone. Also, a desire to understand scripture more deeply. I was flabbergasted! All that time I thought it was me who had that great advice given to my friends when it was amazingly the Holy Spirit working through me, using my gift to edify or uplift another brother or sister in Christ!!!

So here I am at the tender young age of 59 years old writing a book about a relationship with Christ. Many of you who are reading this know me and could certainly tell some tales about me that I may or may not find embarrassing. Trust me that little embarrasses me these days as a result of my walk with Christ I have found that I am just excited to be a tool in His tool bag that He occasionally uses to repair or show love to something or someone who is in need. I truly believe that the most important job we have as His Bride is to love others to Him. What greater blessing of bringing Him Glory can there be? And there is no doubt that He deserves our praise and love above all else.

For we do not wrestle against flesh and blood, but against principalities, against powers, against the rulers of the darkness of this age, against spiritual hosts of wickedness in the heavenly places.

Ephesians 6:12

13 Wrestling

You have an enemy in this world with whom you are wrestling whether you even know it or not. He has been given the power of lies and deception over this world. He was given this power as a result of the choice mankind made and continues to make rejecting the one true living God. He is Satan "the Accuser" also known as the "Father of Lies", "Prince of Darkness", and "Ruler of this World" and it is his desire that you never come to know or have a relationship with God through believing in His Son, Jesus and what He did to give us the gift of eternal life. He is just fine with you not even acknowledging his existence. In fact, he would rather you not even notice him so that he can secretly, cunningly convince you that there is no God much less a need for Him. His business is keeping you distracted from a desire to know God by enticing you with anything and everything the rest of the world is offering as more important for your "happiness" and "success". It really is a battle and whether or not you believe me that is up to you but let me give you fair warning that having read this book, and the things that I have told you leave you no excuse when you stand before God, and we will ALL do that one day.

The battle lines have been drawn. The enemy has been poised and prepared for some time now. Incursions have been ongoing for a while with little resistance. You have to choose sides. There is no neutral territory, nowhere that you or I can escape. We must fight. The time has come to determine which side you are on. If you aren't aware that there is a war going on then you haven't been paying attention. Surely, like the rest of us, you consistently fight daily battles. Perhaps they are with yourself, family, friends, people you don't even know. Circumstances seemingly beyond your control that frustrate you to no end. And you don't even know why! After all, you didn't ask for this crap. You didn't ask to be born, much less have to put up with fighting a battle. What happened to simplicity? Why can't we all just get along? Live and let live? I will tell you why: Choice. It's as simple as that six-letter word. You may not have had the choice whether or not to be born but you have the choice now as to how you will live this gift given to you called life. What are you going to choose? "But I don't want to choose," you say. "Who says I have to choose?" I will tell you who, God. THE God, not A god and HE is the creator of the Universe and our creator. You aren't here by accident, you were planned. You have purpose. Maybe you don't know what your purpose is. I surely don't know the details of your purpose such as vocation, who you should marry, etc. I do know that the most important purpose that you have is a personal, intimate relationship with God. Once again, He is THE God, not just any god of your choosing. God is your creator and knows you best. He knows everything about you, good bad and indifferent.

I don't know you. I don't know what you are going through in your life, what horrors you may have experienced, the sadness, loss, depression, or hopelessness that you may have lived through or are living through now. Perhaps you are just numb to life. You can't find the motivation to see the purpose of life or find true joy, happiness or lasting peace in anything. You want to. You continue to get up every day, go to work or take care of the children or whatever you have to do to survive each day. You may even put on a good front for the world to see so that they will believe that you are doing well, after all you appear to be. But appearances can be deceiving. Something is missing.

You may have done some horrible things in your life that you are ashamed of but because you were surviving you have pushed the pain of those times into the farthest reaches of your mind. But they have a way of sneaking up on you when you least expect them and you have to find some way to alter your reality so that you don't have to face them, it's just too painful. So you take a drink, or pop a pill, or go to a bar and look for someone else who needs to escape their reality and there is a forgetting... for a time. But there always comes that unexpected time again, when you seem to be doing just fine and you sabotage the progress you thought you were making because you don't believe you deserve to be happy, much less at peace and you are tired of trying to appear like you are when you know you aren't. You above many others know that appearances are deceiving. There has got to be more to life than this... something has to be missing.

Perhaps you haven't experienced anything like what I mentioned above, conceivably your life has been basically an ok existence with no extraordinary events that have devastated you. As a whole, in comparison to your contemporaries you consider yourself to be highly successful. After a fairly uneventful childhood, you fell in love in High School, married your sweetheart and soon thereafter began a family. The family appears to be happy and healthy, bills are paid, you have a nice home, vacations every year and a good retirement plan established. You may even attend church, Mass or go to Mosque on a regular basis and are considered a pillar of the community. The problem is that you know it's all a facade. You cannot for the life of you grasp the true peace that you so desire. You pray, you believe in God and you believe that you are doing everything He requires of you, but it feels like God is a stranger or just simply an acquaintance. Even though it would appear that you have everything going perfectly, the appearance is once again deceiving. Something is missing.

There is one truth that I can tell you right now that is the answer and His name is Jesus. He is THE God who planned you, created you and loves you beyond your comprehension. Yes, I know, you may have heard this all before. You have heard the pitch from Preachers or Evangelists. You may even have friends that have shared their stories of faith with you, but you never really bought into it. You played along, played your part, rather well I might add, but nonetheless, secretly you have always known that something wasn't right. You have heard the stories about Jesus. You sing the Christmas carols each year talking about His birth. You celebrate communion, have heard the story of His life and crucifixion. You even accept the belief that He was actually raised from the dead, and still for some reason it doesn't seem real.

The battle is within. We fight with ourselves the most, at least I know I do. I battle doubt and fear. I argue with myself all the time, trying to reason out the difficulties and what I have or have not done to remedy them. It's only when I come off of my high horse and realize that I don't have to fight these battles by myself, God is able and willing to do so. God has not left us defenseless against these battles. As Born-Again Believers in Jesus we are indwelled with the Holy Spirit of the living God! The battles we fight originate through the spiritual realm where Satan and his army use their power of lies and deception to create chaos in our lives. Any form of distraction that can keep us from communing with our Heavenly Father who is ready willing and able to assist us in these battles and fight them single handedly on our behalf if need be. We must prepare ourselves for this spiritual battle on a daily basis. After all no one is promised tomorrow. This does not mean that we don't work and plan for our future. However, the distraction away from God is Satan and his armies biggest aim.

For some people it is hard to comprehend that we are made up of a body, a soul, and a spirit; or really understand what that all means. Well, the body part is not hard to comprehend it is the physical being that houses your soul and spirit. In other words, it's like a computer. A computer has hardware, the actual physical machine with all the wires and microchips, etc. In order for the computer to work it has to have information within it to instruct all of the machinery to work; what operating system, programs etc. These programs etc. are akin to your spirit, it's the information that makes the computer run and it is connected to the electricity that powers it, be it battery or plugged in. Your spirit is the breath of life that God has given to you. Now your soul is the most unique aspect, it is what makes you who you are. All the information of your life, your personality, likes, dislikes, everything that makes you who you are. So in truth who you are is what that information is not the housing in which it resides. You see, your body is only temporary housing. It will one day give out and it will cease to function or die, but the information that it has stored all the days of your life will not simply disappear, because it is eternal.

Here is an example. Say you have a USB thumb drive that is empty and you put it on a postal scale and it weighs about an ounce. Let's say that it can hold up to 10 gigabytes of information. Let's say you spend some bucks and fill it with lots of great applications and programs etc. If you take it back and weigh it again after it is completely full of 10 gigabytes of information do you know what it will weigh? Yep, that's correct, about an ounce. You see the information doesn't weigh anything and in fact you can send it through the air. How many times have you downloaded an app to your phone via WIFI? The point is that your soul is like all of those bytes of information that make up who you are. And the bad news is that you have a fatal virus in your computer that is going to kill it and that virus is like sin. And the only known cure for this virus is the blood of Jesus that was spilled for you and me so that we can have a relationship with Him.

And this connection with God is spiritual, that is why prayer, reading and studying God's word, and fellowship with other Born-Again Believers is so important. As I have stated earlier it is unusual and at first perhaps uncomfortable for someone not used to praying to do so, but understand that your conversations with God are truly and simply that, a conversation. Now it's not like sitting and talking with another human being over a cup of coffee, however it does involve talking to God. And in turn God can and will speak to you, once again not like your friend might over a telephone conversation. God chooses to speak to us through our Spirit because once you are Born Again of His Spirit, the Holy Spirit of God has taken up an eternal residence in you. He is the "Helper" or "Comforter" that Jesus spoke of sending when He returned to Heaven.

Mainly God speaks to us through His word, the Bible which really does hold messages from which to learn how to live our life according to His will. He speaks to us through conversations with other believers who may have experienced similar circumstances that you are experiencing. There are a multitude of ways in which God gets His message through to you as you grow in your relationship with Him. Sometimes He speaks to us in our willingness to simply pause our lives and meditate on who and what He is. There is a scripture that states;

"Be still and know that I am God." Psalms 46:10 (NKJV)

The "be still" part is a Hebrew word "Raphia" and it means to "relax, sink down, withdraw, let go". Good advice, letting go, especially things that we can do nothing about. That's when God shines. He loves to show off, especially for His kids. I have seen it so many times. I have to remind myself, it's by His power, His Spirit, that I am even alive. The longer I live the more I learn about God and it reveals more about myself. How spoiled I am, how impatient I am. I still have trouble with trusting God even with all the multitudes of problems I have encountered that He has brought me through. I struggle with believing His grace covers my stupidity. Grace is unmerited favor from God, meaning I don't deserve it and didn't earn it, He just loves me and gives it to me. One of the scriptures that humbles me the most is:

"For He knows our frame; He remembers that we are dust." Psalm 103:14 (NKJV)

SO, I must rest in the fact that even when I doubt, curse, throw a fit, act like a little spoiled brat, He still has love that covers me. Better yet, He has a love that I truly can't fathom because I am dust. How He loves beyond our human frailty still mystifies me. We learn that for us, loving is a choice; loving someone is a choice we make. It is hard for me to imagine this but it's almost as if God has no choice whether or not to love us because Love is what He is. Think on that for a moment. Perhaps God wanted to give us what He doesn't have. In other words, He can't choose to not love us.

Jesus taught us that our worrying and anxiety about our lives is a waste of good energy that should be rejected. When we focus on God and His promises for our daily lives this depletes the enemy's ability to distract us from the peace God gives and the confidence it inspires. Pay close attention to the words Jesus offers us regarding our worry:

"Therefore I say to you, do not worry about your life, what you will eat or what you will drink; nor about your body, what you will put on. Is not life more than food and the body more than clothing? Look at the birds of the air, for they neither sow nor reap nor gather into barns; yet your heavenly Father feeds them. Are you not of more value than they? Which of you by worrying can add one cubit to his stature?

So why do you worry about clothing? Consider the lilies of the field, how they grow: they neither toil nor spin; and yet I say to you that even Solomon in all his glory was not arrayed like one of these. Now if God so clothes the grass of the field, which today is, and tomorrow is thrown into the oven, will He not much more clothe you, O you of little faith?

Therefore do not worry, saying, 'What shall we eat?' or 'What shall we drink?' or 'What shall we wear?' For after all these things the Gentiles seek. For your heavenly Father knows that you need all these things. But seek first the kingdom of God and His righteousness, and all these things shall be added to you. Therefore do not worry about tomorrow, for tomorrow will worry about its own things. Sufficient for the day is its own trouble." Matthew 6:25-34 (NKJV)

And more importantly Jesus taught us how to pray to our Heavenly Father in a way that approaches all of our needs on a daily basis:

"But you, when you pray, go into your room, and when you have shut your door, pray to your Father who is in the secret place; and your Father who sees in secret will reward you openly. And when you pray, do not use vain repetitions as the heathen do. For they think that they will be heard for their many words.

"Therefore do not be like them. For your Father knows the things you have need of before you ask Him. In this manner, therefore, pray:
Our Father in heaven,
Hallowed be Your name.
Your kingdom come.
Your will be done
On earth as it is in heaven.
Give us this day our daily bread.
And forgive us our debts,
As we forgive our debtors.

And do not lead us into temptation,
But deliver us from the evil one.
For Yours is the kingdom and the power and the glory forever.
Amen." Matthew 6:5-13 (NKJV)

Understanding that living the Christian life is not easy is a surprise for many.

"And he said to all, 'If anyone would come after me, let him deny himself and take up his cross daily and follow me.'" Luke 9:23 (NKJV)

Christianity is not easy. Being a follower of Christ in this world is challenging and difficult but just ask anyone who follows Him, believes in Him, if it's worth it. The answer would be yes. Yes, because the supernatural transformation that occurs when a dead spirit is Born Again and you become a Child of God. Your sins are forgiven! The barrier is down and you have direct communication with God. How it was meant to be from the beginning except this time YOU made the choice. However, even as an adopted child of God filled with the Holy Spirit of God we still reside in a fallen world. Remember that the majority of people that God has lovingly created will still reject Him and choose their own path.

"Enter by the narrow gate; for wide is the gate and broad is the way that leads to destruction, and there are many who go in by it. Because narrow is the gate and difficult is the way which leads to life, and there are few who find it." Matthew 7:13-14 (NKJV)

There are people in our world right now as I type this that are being persecuted because of their faith in Jesus Christ. People literally being put to death, raped, burned alive, buried alive, women's breasts cut off so that they cannot feed their babies, etc. The list of atrocities are long and hard to comprehend, especially because we believe that we should be better human beings in the twenty-first century. Well, forget that. It's getting worse, and will continue to do so. You see this battle has been going on now for quite some time. Satan and his army are getting bolder and influencing more and more, acquiring multitudes of blind followers who don't even recognize that they are worshipping him and not THE God. This blind obedience comes about as mankind actually denies the very existence of THE GOD, and if they do seek a god, a god that they like, one that approves of any lifestyle, attitude, or action that they desire. And this is not knowing THE God.

In fact, even the Church that should represent Christianity and Jesus Christ is in a great spiritual wrestling match, especially here in the United States of America. We have preachers that preach prosperity, positive thinking, instant gratification from their idea of a "Santa Claus" god. They teach a bastardized version of the Gospel and the Bible. Teaching that God wants you to have everything your heart and bodies desire. Don't believe me? How about the multimillionaire men and women who have gotten rich off of the name of Jesus? Is this what Jesus taught, no, not at all; And here's a great quote from the homeless, non-wealthy, Christ;

"But whoever has this world's goods, and sees his brother in need, and shuts up his heart from him, how does the love of God abide in him?" 1 John 3:17 (NKJV)

Jesus cared most about our spiritual health. If your spirit is well, then we are prepared to face the day to day challenges of living in this sin filled, fallen world. When we have preachers and televangelist proclaiming that God wants you to be wealthy, drive a nice car, live in a big fancy house, and have all of your physical desires met, they are not representing the Jesus Christ of the Bible, nor the one that millions know personally. Don't misunderstand me here. There is nothing wrong with money or wealth for that matter. In fact many wealthy people do wonderful good works to help those in need. No, the Bible tells us that it is the "love" of money that is the root of all kinds of evil.

"For the love of money is a root of all kinds of evil, for which some have strayed from the faith in their greediness, and pierced themselves through with many sorrows."
1 Timothy 6:10 (NKJV)

And don't you know that Satan just loves the frustration and confusion this brings to so many. Many will say: "But doesn't God want to bless us with things?" I tell you that perhaps God's blessings and man's idea of blessings are two different things. We tend to give God credit for "blessings" that are material. Many times, these blessings we refer to are a result of our desire for worldly goods, an overabundance of worldly goods in many cases. God wants to bless us with eternal blessings, spiritual blessings, the most important blessings we can obtain. But we live in a fallen world, and we are selfish and spoiled and want what we want when we want it. I know I certainly am guilty of this. But being a child of God gives God the permission, the responsibility, to discipline me. To correct and teach me the way that He desires for me to go:

"And you have forgotten the exhortation which speaks to you as to sons:
'My son, do not despise the chastening of the LORD,
Nor be discouraged when you are rebuked by Him;
For whom the LORD loves He chastens,
And scourges every son whom He receives.'
If you endure chastening, God deals with you as with sons; for what son is there whom a father does not chasten? But if you are without chastening, of which all have become partakers, then you are illegitimate and not sons. Furthermore, we have had human fathers who corrected us, and we paid them respect. Shall we not much more readily be in subjection to the Father of spirits and live? For they indeed for a few days chastened us as seemed best to them, but He for our profit, that we may be partakers of His holiness. Now no chastening seems to be joyful for the present, but painful; nevertheless, afterward it yields the peaceable fruit of righteousness to those who have been trained by it." Hebrews 12:5-11 (NKJV)

If Jesus was our example then we must pay attention to not only what He said but what He did. For example, the importance He placed on prayer. Jesus apparently took prayer very seriously. Look at how Jesus prayed in the Garden of Gethsemane knowing that in a very short time He would be dying a horrible death. The Bible tells us:

"And being in agony, He prayed more earnestly. Then His sweat became like great drops of blood falling down to the ground" Luke 22:44 (NKJV)

The word "earnestly" is "ektenesteron" in the Greek and it means "figuratively stretched out, more intently". Jesus knew what He was about to experience. He knew that He would suffer agonizingly painful physical torture and die on the cross. And He also knew that He, who had never known the separation from God the Father caused by sin, would be taking on the sins of the world. Thereby causing the most egregious suffering He could ever experience. The Bible tells us that:

'For He made Him who knew no sin to be sin for us, that we might become the righteousness of God in Him" 2 Corinthians 5:21 (NKJV)

He also instructed His disciples,
"Watch and pray that you may not enter into temptation. The spirit is indeed willing but the flesh is weak." Matthew 26:41 (NKJV)

That word "watch" in the Greek is "gregoreo" and it means to take heed lest through remission and indolence some destructive calamity suddenly overtake one. Pray that you don't fall into temptation.

Jesus took prayer very seriously. He knows the power that Satan has in this world to lie and deceive millions into living a sinful life separated from God and His righteousness. And even He as God in the flesh understood the power of the continual connection with God the Father through prayer. It is the most powerful weapon in our arsenal against Satan. The early church understood this as it was emphasized by the Apostle Paul who wrote many encouraging and instructive words to the early Born-Again Believers in the first century church. And they are vitally important still today because they give us the tools and weaponry with which we may fight our adversary!

"Therefore take up the whole armor of God, that you may be able to withstand in the evil day, and having done all, to stand.

Stand therefore, having girded your waist with truth, having put on the breastplate of righteousness, and having shod your feet with the preparation of the gospel of peace; above all, taking the shield of faith, with which you will be able to quench all the fiery darts of the wicked one. And take the helmet of salvation, and the sword of the Spirit, which is the word of God; praying always with all prayer and supplication in the Spirit, being watchful to this end with all perseverance and supplication for all the saints— and for me, that utterance may be given to me, that I may open my mouth boldly to make known the mystery of the gospel, for which I am an ambassador in chains; that in it I may speak boldly, as I ought to speak." Ephesians 6:13-20 (NKJJV)

"Rejoice always, pray without ceasing, in everything give thanks; for this is the will of God in Christ Jesus for you." 1 Thessalonians 5:16-18 (NKJV)

"Be anxious for nothing, but in everything by prayer and supplication, with thanksgiving, let your requests be made known to God; and the peace of God, which surpasses all understanding,

will guard your hearts and minds through Christ Jesus."
Philippians 4:6 (NKJV)

So, what do we do? Well, let me tell you. First if you are
reading this and are a Born-Again believer, my brother or sister,
then let me encourage you to seek God like you have never done
before. Make Him the priority for your life and the life of your
family. You are going to find boldness in your witness that you
may have never expected but be encouraged! The Holy Spirit of
the Living God is at work in you and will give you the words to
share with others. God knows the condition of your heart most
importantly and if you feel that there is something that you need to
confess or repent of then do it. Now mind you, you will never be
perfect in this world for God to use you. I believe He uses those of
us who most assuredly are the most imperfect in which to do His
perfect work. Always remember that the Holy Spirit is the one who
in fact is the one who convicts of sin, your willingness to share
your witness is where God's power is made perfect in our
weakness and imperfection. He has only used one perfect person
that I am aware of and that would be His Son seated at His right
hand and waiting patiently for the word from His Dad to come and
get His Bride.

And this is a good place to talk about the importance of
prophecy again because we are living in the time when most of the
prophecies of the Bible will be fulfilled. I am talking about what
Jesus promised to His disciples, that He was going away but that
He was also coming back.

"Let not your heart be troubled; you believe in God, believe also in Me. In My Father's house are many mansions; if it were not so, I would have told you. I go to prepare a place for you. And if I go and prepare a place for you, I will come again and receive you to Myself; that where I am, there you may be also. And where I go you know, and the way you know."

Thomas said to Him, 'Lord, we do not know where You are going, and how can we know the way?'

Jesus said to him, "I am the way, the truth, and the life. No one comes to the Father except through Me." John 14:1-6 (NKJV)

Jesus was speaking of what many Christians refer to as "the Rapture of the Church" and the Church, or body of Born-Again Believers, is also referred to as "The Bride of Christ". This conversation is important because Jesus was talking to His disciples who were familiar with the Jewish tradition of marriage at that time.

The Groom's Father would choose a Bride for His Son and would send His Son to go and meet His chosen Bride. They would "court" or spend time together getting to know one another for a time and then they would discuss the price to be paid by the Groom for the marriage. This also refers to when Jesus was praying in the Garden of Gethsemane as He knew the price He was going to pay, the agony that He was preparing to suffer;

"He went a little farther and fell on His face, and prayed, saying, "O My Father, if it is possible, let this cup pass from Me;

nevertheless, not as I will, but as You will." Matthew 26:39 (NKJV)

When this was agreed upon the Groom and Bride would drink wine from a cup signifying their agreement and entering into a marriage covenant. Then the Groom would return to His Father's house to prepare a room or "place" in which they would live together after their marriage. The Bride during this time was preparing herself for the upcoming wedding, choosing wedding gown, lamps for the wedding etc. . Also making sure the lamps were full because she herself did not know if the Groom would come in the day or night. This refers to the parable of the ten virgins.

"Then the kingdom of heaven shall be likened to ten virgins who took their lamps and went out to meet the bridegroom. Now five of them were wise, and five were foolish. Those who were foolish took their lamps and took no oil with them, but the wise took oil in their vessels with their lamps. But while the bridegroom was delayed, they all slumbered and slept.

"And at midnight a cry was heard: 'Behold, the bridegroom is coming; go out to meet him!' Then all those virgins arose and trimmed their lamps. And the foolish said to the wise, 'Give us some of your oil, for our lamps are going out.' But the wise answered, saying, 'No, lest there should not be enough for us and you; but go rather to those who sell, and buy for yourselves.' And while they went to buy, the bridegroom came, and those who were

ready went in with him to the wedding; and the door was shut."
Matthew 25:1-10 (NKJV)

The honor of deciding when the wedding was to take place was the Father of the Groom's. He would determine the "day and the hour" of the wedding and when He made that decision He would send His Son back to call out to His Bride for her to come with Him back to the Father's house for the marriage feast. I have given a limited explanation here but I suggest you go to this website to discover even more interesting aspects of this tradition. https://free.messianicbible.com/feature/ancient-jewish-wedding-customs-and-yeshuas-second-coming/

"But of that day and hour no one knows, not even the angels of heaven, but My Father only. But as the days of Noah were, so also will the coming of the Son of Man be. For as in the days before the flood, they were eating and drinking, marrying and giving in marriage, until the day that Noah entered the ark, and did not know until the flood came and took them all away, so also will the coming of the Son of Man be. Then two men will be in the field: one will be taken and the other left. Two women will be grinding at the mill: one will be taken and the other left. Watch therefore, for you do not know what hour your Lord is coming. But know this, that if the master of the house had known what hour the thief would come, he would have watched and not allowed his house to be broken into. Therefore, you also be ready, for the Son of Man is coming at an hour you do not expect." Matthew 24:36-44 (NKJV)

Jesus was describing His return not only for His disciples but He knew that these words would be written down for the generations to come, and especially for our generation because He wanted us to be ready. As I stated earlier that prophecies are types of warnings of future events that have yet to unfold. Jesus was in fact prophesying of His return for His Bride. And the Apostle Paul also implied the Rapture in letters to the first century Church as they were hoping that He would return in their lifetime.

"For the Lord Himself will descend from heaven with a shout, with the voice of an archangel, and with the trumpet of God. And the dead in Christ will rise first. Then we who are alive and remain shall be caught up together with them in the clouds to meet the Lord in the air. And thus we shall always be with the Lord. Therefore comfort one another with these words." 1 Thessalonians 4:16-18 (NKJV)

"Behold, I tell you a mystery: We shall not all sleep, but we shall all be changed— in a moment, in the twinkling of an eye, at the last trumpet. For the trumpet will sound, and the dead will be raised incorruptible, and we shall be changed. For this corruptible must put on incorruption, and this mortal must put on immortality. So when this corruptible has put on incorruption, and this mortal has put on immortality, then shall be brought to pass the saying

that is written: "Death is swallowed up in victory."

'O Death, where is your sting?
O Hades, where is your victory?'
The sting of death is sin, and the strength of sin is the law. But thanks be to God, who gives us the victory through our Lord Jesus Christ.

Therefore, my beloved brethren, be steadfast, immovable, always abounding in the work of the Lord, knowing that your labor is not in vain in the Lord." 1 Corinthians 15:51-58 (NKJV)

What you need is Jesus. Who you need is Jesus. You need a personal relationship with Him. You need to know Him intimately and love Him passionately, just as He knows you intimately and loves you passionately. Not passionately in the erotic sense of the word but passionately with love that surpasses all others. He wants to be your first love. He created you for this purpose. You, the one and only, the one that there has never been one like or will ever be another like. He wanted you, wants you, and is ready willing and able to help you accomplish this goal of having this personal relationship with Him and He can become real to you.

Now if you are not a Born-Again Believer in Jesus Christ then let me tell you what to do and what not to do, the latter of which can sometimes be more important. First the fact that you are reading this is evidence of God reaching out to you. Trust me I am not taking credit for what God is doing in your life, I simply know of His power and how He has encouraged me in ways you cannot fathom to do what I am doing by writing this down and making it available to you. The biggest part of my heart has always been to help others learn about THE God I serve, worship, adore, get frustrated with, get angry at, cry with, laugh with, and above all else feel love from. I want you to know that God is real and He loves you so very much. He knows you better than you know yourself. He knows exactly what it is that you are going through. He knows your heartaches, your disappointments, your happiness, your struggles, He knows them ALL, and wants you to come to Him and trust Him with your life. AND He wants you to know that there is not some magical potion that you take, no special dance, no exact words to pray, and it doesn't have to be in a special building lead by anyone in particular associated with any religion. It is between YOU and HIM. He knows your heart. It doesn't matter what you have done in the past. Your future is what concerns Him the most. He knows everything about you and loves you beyond your wildest imagination in spite of your past. He knows your future and loves you in spite of the stupid things you are still going to do. He recognizes that we are human beings with frailties and flesh and blood. He knows about sin, every kind that there is. He hates it with a passion because He knows what it does to us, the ones He loves beyond our comprehension. And I do mean that. We truly can't comprehend how much God loves us. I do know this however, that He loved us enough to come to earth in the flesh as a man, live a sinless life, and pay the price for our sins so that we could have an eternal relationship with Him. This man was Jesus, God in the flesh. The Bible tells us that the wages of sin is death. Death is the price we pay for our sins, and without Christ that death is eternal separation from THE God who made us and wants us to be with Him forever.

And let me stress the importance of finding a church home where you can learn, share, and fellowship with other Born- Again Believers. It is also a place where you can publicly profess your belief and trust in Jesus as your savior. This is what Jesus said concerning publicly professing your faith in Him:

"Therefore whoever confesses Me before men, him I will also confess before My Father who is in heaven. But whoever denies Me before men, him I will also deny before My Father who is in heaven." Matthew 10:32-33 (NKJV)

Finally, I have now come to the end of the information, the tools, the encouragement that I hopefully related to you in a way that is meaningful to you. It is by far an imperfect work however it is full of the word of God which is perfect. The truth contained in this little book can and will change your life if you will place your faith and trust in Jesus and what He has done to make that possible. It's not a fantasy, or fiction, but THE Truth that God created you to know Him and to choose to love Him back and collaborate with Him in this life, with the promise of an eternity spent with Him. But as I have stated many times before, it truly is your choice. It is as simple as that.

This is the last chapter of the main aspect of my book. I have included a final chapter that is about me and my life. I wanted to give you the reader an opportunity to see into who I am and perhaps relate to some of the experiences that I have had in my life. There are no initials behind my name, I am no PhD, or Master of Theology. No, my only qualification for sharing this information with you is my personal relationship with The God of the Universe. So, if you continue to read on I hope you find it of value and perhaps a little humorous at times. It certainly will give you evidence of the power of God in someone's life when they choose to collaborate with Him, make Him Lord of their life and follow His path designed for them. And that someone is of course me.

Be diligent to present yourself approved to God, a worker who does not need to be ashamed, rightly dividing the word of truth.

2 Timothy 2:15

14 This is Me

At 3:10PM on July 4, 1961 I took my first breath. I remember it vividly, yeah right. Who remembers being born? I have been told that I was a beautiful baby but that's what most women say and some men say when they are just being nice. I have seen my baby picture and that's what they were being was nice. And maybe if those jerks hadn't broken into our home and destroyed everything, I would have had more than one baby picture but that's another story. Anyway, there I was kicking and screaming no doubt, I hadn't learned how to yell yet, making myself known to my loving mother and whoever else was around. I am quite sure that I was hungry after all isn't that what babies mostly cry about? I was born in the early 60's so the father being in the delivery room was unheard of at the time but that didn't matter anyway because my father was in prison. I still to this day am not completely sure what for, regardless, he wasn't there so my mother had to be the one to welcome me into the world.

Now don't get me wrong, I hold no malice against my father for not being there. I am even now as I write this kind of sad, for him and my mother. They have both passed away now but you know how it is when you are remembering things. Which is really strange considering all I cared about at the time was food and being warm like I was just moments before I was forced into this crazy, cold world. I mean no one even thought about asking me if

I wanted to leave the nice warm space I had been inhabiting. All my needs met without even a whimper. But then again who gets the choice as to whether or not they are born? In case you are wondering I am very glad that I was. Life is hard, but the longer I live the more I know it's worth it. Took a while but I think I finally get it. Of course, I haven't done it on my own. Who does?

My Grandfather often told the story of me being just four days old when he came in the house and my mother was feeding me cereal. He asked my mother if she was trying to kill me. Of course, whoever heard this story for the first time always laughed, probably because I was a fat kid. She wasn't trying to kill me by the way, she just couldn't breast feed me because of inverted nipples or something like that. Anyway, I lived, as is evidenced by the fact I am writing this now. I wasn't always a fat kid, I started out a pretty average size for my age. There were mitigating circumstances that assisted my metabolism into giving up the fight.

My Father was a dairyman, builder, and primarily an alcoholic. He was in the Marines during World War II stationed on Guadalcanal and although he had dabbled in alcohol during his high school years, I believe the alcoholism didn't get its undying grasp on him until he faced those horrors of war. Thankfully he wasn't a violent alcoholic, quite the contrary. He was known for giving you the shirt off of his back, often to his own detriment and subsequently his family also. He fought the battle until the age of 43 when on a cold winters night in 1968 he kissed a train and departed this mortal coil. Needless to say, this had a devastating effect on my mother, my 11-year old sister, and me, all of 6 years old.

I don't have a lot of memories of my father. None of me riding on his shoulders, or wrestling matches. I do recall riding in the car on the way to my Grandmother's house and singing. I remember him singing. He had a beautiful voice. Maybe that's one of the reasons I pursued music as a vocation when I got older. That and the fact that he and my mother had genetically gifted me with a good voice also. The little things we recall. As a parent I have to watch myself, although I do it rather poorly, what little things I am imparting to my children's memories. God please help them to be good and beneficial!

My Mother was a nurse, a very good one. There is no doubt that there is a calling to that profession. She had the heart for it. I was the beneficiary throughout my life of meeting some of her grateful patients that had been under her care, that showered her with love and affection. And she loved it so. In fact that's how she met my father. He had been in an automobile accident and broken his neck and she was his nurse. Love at first sight? I don't know but one thing led to another and they got hitched. Not sure what the recovery time is for a broken neck but let's just say he had to take the neck brace off for the wedding pictures. People did things rather quickly back then; perhaps too quickly. You see, my father was an alcoholic when they wed and I am not sure my mother fully understood what she was getting herself into. I am glad she did, mind you, because I wouldn't be here, however, I wish I could have prevented some of the pain that came with his disease. Like him getting blind drunk on the first night of their honeymoon. I was never given the details because my mother, although very honest and forthright, thought it best not to sully what little memory I did have of my father with them. I can only imagine what she endured. There is however, a funny story about their honeymoon. Remember my father was still using a neck brace and one morning they received a wakeup call from the front desk of the hotel in which they were honeymooning. When my mother reached over for the phone, she dropped it on her eye which gave her a nice shiner. So, when they told people that they were on their honeymoon and people looked at them, her with a black eye and him with a neck brace, well, you can imagine the looks they got!

All those decades ago alcoholism had not been designated as a disease. There were various treatments for the "weakness" and thank God for Bill W. Although even good old Bill and the twelve steps weren't enough for dear old dad. And his mother, my Grandmother, hated his "weakness". She believed that the incentive treatment should work for him. What I mean is that she thought that if she and my Grandfather could come up with the right combination of gifts to give him the incentive to stop drinking, he would stop. That started out ok but then when he fell off of the wagon, the "gifts" were taken back. And I am not talking about small gifts. You see my father's parents had money. Not a lot of it but they were considered "well to do" in that era. Not millionaires by any stretch but having worked hard and invested wisely, they could afford to buy a house and some land and give it to my parents. Perhaps there was still a mortgage on the property I am not sure of all of the details, however, I am familiar with the stories.

Like when my Grandparents bought a nice little home out in the country on a little chunk of land and "gave" it to my parents. They painted and fixed it up, planning to move in. Then my daddy "fell off of the wagon"; goodbye house. You disappointed us again so we are going to give it to your sister. So, my parents lived with that. Ok, let's try again. Grandparents buy a big chunk of land with the dream of one day having all three children and their families living on it along with them, kind of like the "Dallas" nighttime soap opera. So, Mom and Dad move out onto the property which is laden with pine trees and therefore a wealth of cash to be made through "pulp wood". They lived on that, Dad worked the land, for a while, then as it would happen, he got drunk again. Bye-bye land, and dream. See how that incentive treatment didn't work? Not to mention how it damaged my father's relationship to his mother, the woman who gave him life, who rejected him because of his "weakness". I am not sure, but isn't that considered "conditional love"?

Needless to say, I believe my parents had had enough and decided to move away. Let's see, how far can you get if you are in South Carolina and want to put some distance between you and the pain of rejection? How about moving to California? Apparently, that sounded good. So, they up and moved to California. After all my mother was the responsible one with an ability to make a living being a nurse. I loved her stories of the people she met and the fact that they lived not too far from the first McDonalds where they could get cheap burgers. Not real sure what my Dad did there, other than drink; my poor Mom. She did love the man. But enough became enough and I believe the incentive train was up and running again so they moved back to SC. They would live in different homes, helped out by my Grandparents. They had my sister, then unexpectedly me 4 years and 7 months after my sister. I remember my mother telling me of her visit to the doctor. "I don't know how this happened!", she said crying. "Well," the doctor told her while looking out the window, "there isn't a star in the East, and I know you aren't a virgin". I say I was unexpected and I was, but not unwelcome. I was loved, we were just a normal family who fights their battles. Alcoholism was a serious foe.

My father was raised in a "Christian" home, although he never seemed to find his direction, his purpose. At one point he thought he had been called to be a preacher so he moved our little family up to Massachusetts. There was a little Bible college up there and I think he thought that would be a great place to work on his "weakness". Well, let's just say that we were only there for a few months. We moved into a big house that was more or less an old farm house turned into a "duplex". And that would be a place that would devastate my life. I was only three years old for God's sake. What kind of animal sodomizes a three-year old? Apparently, a nice enough man who ingratiates himself to a child's parents who are going to school and working and could use a little help with the kids. "Sure, I will be glad to watch them for you." God only knows if the sick person abused my sister, I don't think so because I believe he was just into little ole me.

Of course, sexual abuse is as old as mankind. It certainly happened back then, not nearly as much as today, or perhaps I am being naive. Perhaps it did, we just didn't find out about it. Regardless, it certainly did a number on me. I think that's when I started eating a little more. I know it's when I started crapping in my pants. Today we would want to know what the problem going on if our three-year old is standing in the corner trying to hold in his crap without success. I think it was because I didn't like the feeling of taking a crap, because I didn't like the feeling. I wonder why? But nature takes over of course. My family got used to it. Of course, it was because I was "lazy," or whatever reason that seems "reasonable" to parents in the chaos of alcoholism, trying to provide a living, and the Massachusetts winter into which we had moved. Oh yes, there was snow. Couldn't they have moved there in the Springtime at least? Maybe in warmer weather that sick abuser wouldn't have been able to keep me inside and well… wishful thinking. Water under the bridge.

So that was when I was three. Daddy got drunk again, we left Massachusetts and went back to SC. Moved onto some more "pulp wood" land where my father would attempt to straighten up and make a go of it again. Mama was always working. Well, not always. The land we lived on in a trailer had a couple of small "lakes" on it. Great fishing, I loved fishing with a cane pole from the bank; great memories of that. Even some pictures of us doing so. We made friends with a nice family with a teenage son who also liked little boys. He was just another "friend" of the family who endeared himself to our family and was allowed to watch over us when our parents were busy trying to provide for us. It's a familiar story, too many sadly enough. Don't get me wrong here. I am not seeking sympathy. I just want to give you some understanding. Everybody has crap they go through in their lives. I am just stupid enough to share with everybody apparently. You learn to laugh through the pain, God knows I have shed enough tears about it, not a victim but a victor.

Ok so where were we. Oh yeah, living on the lake being abused by a trusted family friend, still crapping my pants. I wonder why? I guess I am writing this for all the family members who may end up reading this and will now know why I often smelled so horrible. I am also sharing all of this so you can understand that even though God loves us and is sovereign His will here on earth is not always done. It's the way it works because of the freedom of choice He lovingly gave us. I know that it wasn't His will that I suffered sexual abuse. I know that He could have intervened at any time and I am not sure that He didn't. I firmly believe that God allows us to go through trials and pain because He can see the end result. His amazing ability to turn something horrible into something good. So, I have learned through my many years of a close relationship to Him to trust that He has the power to take something as horrible as sexual abuse and turn it into something good and beneficial. It's a promise in His word that I hold tightly to especially when there are circumstances beyond my comprehension occurring in my or some loved one's life.

"For we know that all things work together to those who love God, to those who the called according to His purpose." Romans 8:28 (NKJV)

And I am praying as I write this that perhaps my struggle will help someone else who has also suffered an experience like this.

But let's get back to my history. The lake thing didn't last very long either. The woods caught on fire. Not a good thing when you need the trees for pulp wood. Subsequently, we moved in with my father's parents in their big house in town. Daddy was allowed to stay there, if he wasn't drinking. The house was a great big old house built into a hill. It was two stories that had access to outside upstairs and down. It was a great big "duplex" in many ways. Amazing how my Grandparents were the only ones who lived their initially. You would have had to have known my Grandmother. She was "highfalutin" so to speak. And they were gracious enough to have pity on us and take us in, understanding my father had his "weakness".

My Grandparents bought this big red brick house when they moved "up" a little in society. My Grandfather was a dairyman and later a builder and had made a name and a reasonably good reputation in the community. He had worked hard to make the business successful and they were enjoying the fruits of their labor. They moved from a big farm outside the city limits to just inside of them. They sold the farm or developed it themselves I can't rightly remember. Regardless they made a little chunk of money and bought this house on two acres in the city limits.

Now my Grandmother was a "Southern" lady and for all of you Southerners out there you will understand what I mean. She was refined and "genteel". She had named the farm where they had lived before "Hope Hill" so it was fitting that she also name this new home. The name she chose was "Rose Manor" which was fitting as she was a lover of roses. In fact, because of her work with various Garden clubs and Society/Charity organizations and probably because she would wear a rose in her "bosom," she became known as "The Rose Lady". She loved roses and she had a lot of them, God knows I helped her plant enough of them! She was locally famous and she loved it. She was however a little too caught up in the opinion's others had about her and our family which is probably why she hated the fact that daddy was a "drunk".

Like I stated earlier, this house was a big house to begin with and they made it even bigger. They built on a big room the length of the entire downstairs with a kitchen on one end. There was a purpose in this as their extended family was growing and my Grandmother loved to entertain the Garden Club, Rose Society, Women's Temperance Union, etc., you get the picture. Many times, the Christmases were thirty or more people sitting down to eat at two giant tables pushed together. It was a BIG room. Also, another big bedroom was added to the downstairs which in turn made it an independent apartment so to speak. The upstairs and downstairs had private entrances. This was great for us when we came to live with them because it gave us all a little bit of separation when needed. The house consisted of a kitchen upstairs with an eat in area. From there you entered into a formal living room/dining room area. This was also used as a kind of "den". I didn't know what a "den" was growing up. We only had living rooms according to "Grandma." This was what I called her which she didn't particularly like. She wanted the more formal "Grandmother" title. Her name was Gladys so she actually preferred GG for Grandmother Gladys.

Anyway, the upstairs was more of a "refined" space full of beautiful antiques and a portrait of Grandad over the fireplace in the living room. Of course, it was filled with beautiful antiques and fancy named pieces; Oriental or Egyptian rugs, etc. I guess when we moved in, they put their TV in the room which apparently wasn't there before because this was such a refined space. But we are talking the 60's here so TV's and multiple TV's back then were a sign of opulence so that certainly pleased GG. Now please don't misunderstand me when I am talking about my Grandma. She was a very loving lady, a loving Grandma. She was beautiful, personable, gracious, lady. Yes, she had her faults and opinions but she could handle opposition and any confrontation with a very definite "style" all her own. And boy did she have style. I didn't grow up around desks, it was called the secretary. And I still don't understand what a "credenza" is. But there is a purpose in telling you these little side stories. It is important for me to relate to you, information about who I am and the influences in my life that brought me to where I am now. And I hope it allows you time to reflect upon your life and the conflicts and struggles you may have encountered. And hopefully you will grow in your relationship to Him, to trust Him and let Him turn ashes into beauty.

"To console those who mourn in Zion, To give them beauty for ashes, The oil of joy for mourning, The garment of praise for the spirit of heaviness; That they may be called trees of righteousness, The planting of the Lord, that He may be glorified." Isaiah 61:3 (NKJV)

Let's get on with "Rose Manor". Off of the upstairs big living/dining area was a large stairway that led to the downstairs. Across from that was the large formal entrance to the home, (which was rarely used) and known as the "foyer". It had a marble floor and the huge wooden door was imported from Italy or Spain or somewhere. Also, in the foyer was a Grandmother clock, not Grandfather mind you, Grandmother. It was smaller and more refined but just like Grandma, you could hear it when it chimed throughout the whole house. Just off of the foyer was the "music parlor". Now this was THE most refined room in the house. It was one of my favorite rooms to come and just sit. It had a baby grand piano, two really cool big blue chairs that would swallow a little kid up, even a fat little kid. Grandma called them the "William and Mary" chairs, I think after king and queen somebody. I would have thought they would have been called the "William and Gladys" chairs but that's just me. They had beautiful carved wood on them and were covered in some type of velvet. Oh, and they had these little red- velvet covered footrest which for me as a kid were an added bonus. And I was told that they had once belonged to the stage actress Fanny Brice. The chairs sat in front of the fireplace that had this really ornate white wooden mantle. On the mantle were these crystal and brass candelabras. Over the mantle was another portrait and that was, you guessed it, Grandmother herself. Marble topped coffee tables, mahogany "fancy-shmancy" love seat, and one big red satin covered sofa. Starting to get the picture here? This was some house to grow up in.

There was not one painted wall in the house. It was either wallpaper or real wooden paneling. Well, there were the ceilings, they were painted. I digress. Off of the music parlor and through French doors was the "veranda". Nothing had a regular name like "porch". This space was the top of the huge room that was added on downstairs. It was filled with wicker furniture and those old-time metal rocker sofas. Then also off of the music parlor was my Grandparents room, well I should say Grandma's room because there was absolutely nothing manly about it. It was mostly done in baby blue colors from the ceiling to the wallpaper to the carpet. Two single red cherry canopy beds, and a little delicate velvet covered rocker. Oh, and a fireplace and another big white wooden mantle with picture of the Madonna and Child over it. Can I just tell you that this whole upstairs was screaming to my little body to come and play...NOT! But wait, I forgot the bathroom! Oy vey! This place was a home within itself. It was white too, what's up with the white? My Grandparents had not foreseen that their little grandkids would be living with them I guess but then again is that really ever the plan? Let's get back to the bathroom. White tiled floor, big white bathtub with giant mirrors on all three sides. A southern lady's pride and joy no doubt. I loved standing in front of the mirror by the sink that was opposite those mirrors over the tub. I could see a zillion of me. And there were mirrors everywhere; In the walls, on the walls. Downstairs there was a whole wall that was a mirror, that was the library and my bedroom, I will get to that later.

Coming back out of my Grandma's bedroom was the stairway leading downstairs. It was carpeted which saved my butt many times, literally. Off of the landing at the bottom of the stairs to the left was the scariest room in the house, the basement. Remember I told you that the house was built into a hill, well this basement wasn't like a regular basement you would think of. It was on the same level as the downstairs. Well, actually one step up from the downstairs. It had this giant scary furnace and pipes going hither and yon and duct work and spider webs. It had the breaker panel and old unused furniture and the washer and dryer. Now that was fun, going into this scary room to get something out of the dryer or put something in the washer. Probably because there was this door up behind the dryer. Just a door that I didn't know what was behind it. It wasn't a regular size door it was like a small little closet door but we never used it because it wasn't easy to get to because of the dryer. I didn't find out what was behind that door till years later when I accidentally set the house on fire in the basement. Thank God we got it out but not before it did terrible smoke damage to the house and wrecked the basement. We had to clean out the burned-up stuff in the basement and while we were at it might as well see what was behind that door. To our surprise it held the remains of Jimmy Hoffa; Just kidding. It did have some old junk but nothing much to speak of. I was at least glad to find out what was behind the mystery and the spiders. Oh yes, in a house this old, I don't care how refined it was, you had spiders, and roaches. Oh, my goodness I could spend pages telling about dealing with bugs; maybe later.

So, come out of the basement and step down off of the landing and to your left was another big bathroom. Tile out the yingyang and did I mention mirrors? Oh yes, you could enjoy watching yourself sitting on the toilet with ease. What were these people thinking? I guess like my Grandad used to say, "Like the old lady who kissed the cow. Everybody to their own notion!"

This bathroom had two entrances, one off of my mother and sister's room which was pink and purple with flowery wall paper. A big king size bed, well, two single beds pushed together with a big white wrought iron headboard. Purple carpet, well almost all of it was that is until my cousin was spending the night and got sick and puked all over it. I guess stomach acid can make dye change colors. Once again, I digress. Anyway, my mother and sister shared this room after my dad died. My sister and I shared the library/bedroom/giant wall mirror room until then. Out of their room was the big downstairs living room, or I guess had I known the term I would have referred to it as the den. It was paneled floor to ceiling in wood paneling, and I mean the real deal not that fake stuff. You know the knotty pine kind with interesting shapes in it. This is where we kept our television; our tv room, with a big three-piece sectional, flowery, sofa. Two big leather chairs, or maybe they were faux leather (the shame), and a wonderfully braided rug, you know the kind that goes around and round from the middle to the ends. The kind a little kid with some Hot Wheel cars can spend hours on in front of the console television. Oh, and let's not forget that we needed a floor to ceiling mirror behind the television. I did love that mirror I guess because of its manliness. It was framed in this beautiful wood and of course I could watch myself and the tv at the same time. Learning to mimic is a serious job.

Another big fireplace in that room, a real wood burning fireplace unlike the gas logs upstairs. Loved that fireplace until Christmas when my Grandad would threaten to make the fire too large for Santa to come down the chimney. And atop that fireplace, above the dark wooden mantle, (I know, you thought it would be white didn't you) hung a painting of their former home, the farm, "Hope Hill". It was a beautiful painting that had been commissioned by a local artist. I can remember many moments just staring at that painting waiting on the cow's to "moo" or the dog to bark. They never did, only in my imagination, which was on overload living in this house. And in one corner was this beautiful built in wooden desk and bookshelf. It had little pigeon holes for letters and little drawers and big drawers. Another fun place for a kids imagination to run wild.

Off of the living room and through two giant folding louvered doors was THE room. The giant room where most of the entertaining was done. It was the length of the entire downstairs. At one end was our kitchen which was a nice size in itself with a big island in the middle. The room was where we did our "formal" dining. You know, Sunday dinner or when we had company. And at the other end of the room was a space my Grandma christened the "courting corner" for my sister's enjoyment when she got older. It was where we put up the big Christmas tree and the family would gather around for Grandma to pass out all the presents. It was the room that the Garden Club would enjoy on special occasions. Where any number of her Society groups would come to meet. And where I and my sister would throw a few parties when we got older.

The only thing that was more prevalent about this house than the mirrors was the windows. Oh, my word, did this house have windows. BIG windows, one that was floor to ceiling that I knew I was going to accidentally break but thankfully never did. I would still be paying for it if I had. So, there were windows, and windows get dirty over time. Guess who learned how to clean windows growing up? Bingo! And French doors off of this room leading to this really big set of stairs going down the hill. Of course, I say really big because in my mind's eye everything about this house was huge. I guess I still see it from my childlike perspective.

Off of this room was my room or what it was designed to be, the library. The reason being was that there was another built in wooden desk and bookshelf thingy, like it was too far to walk to the other one. And lots of other built in bookshelves. Two big louvered door closets and big wooden cabinets. And then there was this giant floor to ceiling mirror, like you were in a dance recital hall or something. And when I say floor to ceiling, I failed to mention that these weren't eight-foot ceilings, more like ten. Now this room wasn't designed to be a bedroom but it was functional probably because of the two closets. It was one of the rooms with the knotty pine ceilings with all the little "faces" in those knots. Believe me, they were faces, at least they were to me growing up in this dance recital hall library. The room had doors everywhere. Not regular doors, those bifold louvered doors with little windows on top. Why you ask? I guess so that the burglars or ghosts could see in on me at night as I was trying to go to sleep with the light on. Oh, and did I mention the giant window in that room? Yep, another one, but of course it had this giant curtain that I could pull at night to keep the boogie man from seeing in.

However, it was spooky in the daytime. There was this big beautiful palmetto tree right outside the window that had the habit of gnarling it self's shadows into ominous shapes. The shadows would keep the knotty pine faces company when I wasn't around.

In front of the louvered doors, I guess to block it off because the passage way wasn't necessarily needed, was a cedar chest. To the left of that was another "secretary," or big bookshelf, desk thingy with bookshelves inside it behind glass covered ornate wooded doors. It became a desk when you folded down the front of it and inside of it was another set of those little letter pigeon holes and little drawers; just another giant plaything for a kid. And on the floor, covering the hardwood, was another of those wonderful braided rugs. I had two twin beds that sat under the bookshelves and in front of the wooden cabinets. I also thankfully had a big dresser with its own mirror in front of the ballet mirror. I liked the bed on the right, because it was the farthest away from the window and closest to the nearest escape route in the event the knotty pine faces decided to literally come visit. Now as I think about it, it wasn't such a good idea to sleep with the light on because I would wake up and right above where I was sleeping was one of those faces staring back at me.

This was the house I grew up in and the reason I share it with you is because this is where my relationship with God began. Seriously think about that. Wouldn't you want to know THE God who could protect you from the knotty pine people? This was the house where on a cold February morning I was awakened by a house full of people talking, and crying. Where my Mama took me to our bathroom and sat down and told me that my father was dead. It was into that faux leather chair in front of the roaring anti-Santa fireplace that I retreated not fully understanding the why of it all. It was there that a well-intentioned minister and friend of our family came, gently put his hand on my knee, and told me that I was now the man of the family, at the tender age of six years old.

We continued to live in this house after my father died at the insistence of my Grandparents who knew the difficulties my mother already had basically being a single parent and working all the time. It was truly a blessing for our little family because my sister and I got the benefit of spending a lot of time with our Grandparents who we loved very much. Of course, it wasn't always peache's and cream, it's hard for families no matter how much they love each other to live in peace all the time but thankfully those rough patches were far and few in between.

It was there, within those "umpti-leven" walls, with all the mirrors and the windows, that I learned to look at myself and within. At the same time learning to look outside at the great big world and question... and choose. It was there that I learned it was ok to question, argue, fight with, struggle, cry and laugh with this God who had taken my father and thereby made me the man of our little family, and where I had learned ABOUT God. I had heard and been taught a wealth of "Bible" stories. I had been to Sunday school and big Church, heard the preacher teach, been pinched when I acted up along with being given "the mother look". But the stories weren't enough. The teaching answered some questions but I wanted more. I wasn't satisfied with knowing ABOUT God. I thought I knew God, after all He had helped me find one of my toys when I asked him to. When I prayed at night and asked Him to bless me and my family, I believed that He was. I knew the story about Jesus and I accepted that it must be true, because I trusted that my family wouldn't lie to me, and neither would the people at church. And yet something wasn't complete, something was missing in this otherwise fulfilled little world in which I lived.

Then one day in my tenth year of life, I was nine years old but living in my tenth year of life, which I say to drive my daughter crazy, anyway, I was nine years old. It was a Sunday much like any other Sunday. Nothing notable other than something the preacher said grabbed my attention. I am not sure if that is a good enough description. It was more like something grabbed my heart, my soul, the very essence of who I am. I had listened before and thought I heard, but this time was different, this time I REALLY HEARD. When the preacher said that sin was keeping us from knowing God. That everyone was a sinner because everyone had sinned. There wasn't anyone who hadn't, except one person. He was saying that Jesus was that someone. Now I had been taught that Jesus was God's Son, and that He died on the cross for our sins and I accepted that, but it was just more or less a story to me. I guess I hadn't really personalized the fact that I had a responsibility in the equation. It wasn't just sin that was keeping me from a relationship with God; It was MY sin; Me. I had done wrong. It wasn't Adam and Eve. It wasn't my parents or Grandparents or anyone other than me. I was responsible for the separation between me and God. And Jesus was the answer to this. My heart was telling me this in a way I had never experienced before. I can't explain it except to say that I knew that this was the truth. There was something, better yet someONE, speaking to my heart. The preacher asked if there was anyone in the congregation that wanted to know Jesus, that wanted to get saved and I found myself walking to the front of the church and kneeling down. The preacher bent down and whispered to me,

"Do you want to ask Jesus to forgive you of your sins? Do you believe He died for you, for your sins?" Something tweaked inside me. Tears filled my little nine-year old eyes and I realized MY SINS. I had always heard that Jesus died for the whole world's sins. That it was a done deal for everyone. But I was right and wrong at the same time. He did die for the sins of the world. But the relationship with God wasn't possible unless I received the gift of forgiveness. The FREE gift. It was there for the taking, all I had to do was choose to ACCEPT it. I mean really, what good is a gift that you never open or ACCEPT? Through tear stained cheeks and swollen eyes I told the preacher "yes". It didn't matter that I was just nine years old. My sins were relative to my age. I mean how big a sinner could I have been at nine? The point is that it didn't matter, ANY sin was keeping me from what I longed for, a personal relationship with God. All I can tell you is that when I uttered that word "yes," my life changed eternally.

That's when the miracle happened, well I call it a miracle, and I am sure everyone who has become a child of God by being born again of His Spirit, calls it that too. It is when God comes to live IN you. My sins were forgiven and not just my past sins. ALL of my sins were forgiven, even the ones I had yet to commit and there would certainly be a quite a few. Now there are those in the Christian religion that disagree with me about this. And I am quite sad for them because they don't fully grasp God's grace, His love. You see, I was given a gift from God. He knew that I was incapable of ever being good enough, sin free so to speak, without His assistance. I could never earn it, much less deserve it, and He certainly doesn't take back a gift. No, those who don't believe that you are saved once and forever apparently believe that they are going to have to work to earn it. How sad to believe that God is like that; No, Satan is like that. He is the liar that deceives even children of God that they have to do good works to earn their way into heaven. Don't you buy into that. Good works are something you do as a result of becoming a child of God. It's a natural aspect of the miracle. You take on the traits of your father. It's a natural outpouring of God's love to others THROUGH you. Of course, you don't want to sin, who does? But facing the facts, that we are still attached to our flesh and blood bodies, we are going to sin. Doesn't mean we should aim for it, no quite the contrary. It is with God's help that we resist sinning. It's a matter of recognizing that God's love is what it's all about. The whole thing is because of His love and desire for us. It's as simple as receiving a gift.

Let me say that becoming a Child of God is a wonderful, supernatural experience, but it is not a rose garden, and I am familiar with rose gardens. Your eternity is secure. You can't lose it and this makes Satan very angry. He knows that he can't have your soul so he is going to do everything in his power to stifle your life because his desire is to steal, kill, and destroy, especially children of God. So if you are thinking that life began to take on the hue of rose colored glasses that would be naive. In short, this amazing, eternal, supernatural occurrence began my lifelong battle with the father of lies who is a mighty foe. Recall the chapter on "Wrestling"! But my Heavenly Father is almighty and the fact that He lives in me gives me access to that power to resist and defeat Satan in his many attempts to destroy my life and witness.

Knowing about God and knowing Him personally are two very different things. Going to church is a good thing but it doesn't make you a Christian. After all, going to McDonalds doesn't make you a Big Mac does it? So, the most important aspect of my creation had been achieved with my acceptance of Jesus into my life. It gave me the relationship with God that we both desired. It's why He created us in the first place, to have a relationship with us and share His limitless love with us. Once you experience this you will know what I mean. There is a supernatural aspect that lets you know that this is THE TRUTH, not my truth or someone else's truth but the truth that is God. This is why God tells us in His word that He is a jealous God. He is not jealous as in "you will hurt my feelings if you choose another god." He is jealous for us to worship Him and Him only because all other gods are false and the truth is not in them. They only lead to destruction and eternal death and separation from Him, and this is not His desire for us. But if it's not His desire then why does He allow it you ask? Remember that we have been given the choice, without it, we are puppets. It has always been about us and our choice to either choose Him back and love and obey Him for our own good, or reject Him and suffer eternal consequences.

At nine years old I still had a life in front of me. Although, at that young age I was ready to go to heaven and be with God forever. Beam me up Jesus! After all childlike faith is exactly what it says, childlike. All the stories of the Bible took on a new meaning to me now. They seemed to resonate within me differently for some reason. I no longer thought of them as just stories, they all of a sudden represented real people who had lived and experienced those amazing things. They had fought physical and spiritual battles with the power of the living and true God fighting with and for them. I too wanted to experience this, perhaps not in ways that would be written down for future generations but because feeling and knowing the power of God now lived within me gave me the desire to make a difference even in my own little world; an eternal difference. But I still had lots of questions that I wanted answers to.

The first pressing answer that I wanted to understand was, where did God come from? Not an unusual question for a nine - year old, for that matter many adults ask the same question. I remember vividly as if it were yesterday, standing in my mother's room staring at my hand and wondering how everything came into being, especially God. I mean, everything has a beginning, right? My finite mind could not comprehend that God has always been, was not created, didn't just appear out of nowhere but has always existed. That one still causes problems for so many. The answer for me was rather simple and yet profound. I know it was without a doubt a God given answer, just as it has been for every Born-Again believer in Jesus. The answer is faith. The Bible tells us;

"Now faith is the substance of things hoped for, the evidence of things not seen." Hebrews 11:1 (NKJV)

The substance of things hoped for… I sure was hoping that what I believed was true, I was wanting to know that all those stories I had been taught as a child were true. I was hoping that Jesus was real and that he really did die on a cross two thousand years ago for my sins. I hoped that he really did rise from the grave proving that He was God's Son and securing a way for me to know God. And the evidence was that the unseen God had come to physically, spiritually, live within me as a result; Faith.

"So, then faith comes by hearing, and hearing by the word of God." Romans 10:17 (NKJV)

The reason all of those Bible stories took on a new meaning to me was because they were the word of God. His word is supernatural and has the ability to break through the lies and the deception that Satan continually produces in the world. You see, since the beginning of time Satan has deceived mankind, beginning with Adam and Eve and continually to this very day. But God's word is the truth, it is light that shines in the darkness and overcomes it. The darkness that is in the heart of mankind because of sin. The darkness that causes us to seek the light and the truth that is only found in the one true living God. Hearing these words growing up began to shine light into the darkness of my life. I had no idea that it was doing this, but God has always had the plan to make himself known to mankind and to make a way for him to have the relationship with Him and this is dependent on faith.

And all of this is true and wonderful, but I was only nine years old. I still had my life in front of me and choices to make, and sadly, regrettably, I would make many that would have consequences that were unwelcome. You see becoming a born-again believer in Jesus Christ is truly a simple thing, as simple as receiving a gift that is offered. Living a Christian life is most assuredly a challenging effort as you will see from the rest of my story.

Childhood can be challenging regardless of whether it was this so-called happy childhood, or unhappy Childhood, or just an average childhood. I would say mine was not average because my father died when I was six and we lived with my grandparents. There were no major incidents that happened other than the sexual abuse, I was a kid that played kickball, enjoyed the families get together's at Christmas, and birthdays, and went to school. Enjoyed school until the chaos of segregation and busing hit our area. This was the late 60's and early 70's in the deep South where Jim Crowe was ending but the after effects were lingering. My sister who is about five years older than me was going to be bussed to a school that was experiencing a lot of riots and upheaval so my mother and grandparents determined that private school would be the best alternative for my sister and me. So, from fourth grade until eighth grade I attended a private school. This was beneficial from the standpoint of education because the demand for performance was greater and therefore my learning was increased beyond that of the Public-School system. But when my sister graduated from high school it was no longer feasible for me to continue on in private school, so I began my eighth-grade year in public school once again.

This was a dramatic change for me not only from the standpoint of race relations but simple societal relations. In the private school system mainly because parents paid out of their pockets for their children's education and there was a higher expectation for return on the investment the attitude and day to day performance of the children was different. And although there was a certain amount of peer pressure and light bullying, when there were problems between kids it was handled quickly by school administration as well as parents at home. And once again I was a fat kid no matter what school I went to and kids can be mean everywhere. So even in the private school I endured my share of not so nice unwanted attention. That is until I began my eighth-grade year in the public school.

Now the friends that I had at church and that group in general were never unkind to me as a fat kid and this gave me opportunity to allow my personality to blossom and flourish. I discovered I was funny and smart and attracted a lot a friend's during this time. Whereas I blossomed at church, I wilted at school. Perhaps it was because I was very smart in school and also was the vulnerable fat kid, I faced many challenges. So, I was faced with a threat of bodily injury if I wouldn't do someone's homework or help them cheat on a test by copying off of my paper. And there were times when I had had enough and would face the physical pain of a kick or a punch because I would no longer comply. There were visits to the principal's office and even the law had to get involved one time but through it all, because of the love and support I received from my family and friends at church, I had learned to trust that God would see me through it, and he did. Don't get me wrong, it was far from easy, but looking back I can't imagine how it must've been for other kids if you did not have that relationship with God like I did.

The Bible doesn't say much about Jesus and his teenage years, in fact it simply says that he grew in favor with man and God. My theory on that is that it is easier to believe that God raised him from the dead than it is to believe that he lived a sinless teenage life. Of course, I say that in jest and truly believe that he did not only because he was God's son but because of the intense relationship he had with God the Father and that he displayed in his public life. And I'm talking about the importance of prayer, or the intimate communication with God that it affords. Life can be difficult no matter what age you are but if you have lived through them, the teenage years are most assuredly some of the most challenging years of your life. The transition from childhood to adulthood, the need to establish independence, acceptance from your peers, self-confidence, and self-control are some of these challenges. But having an intimate relationship with God during this trying time is a wonderful benefit. And I reaped this benefit most definitely because of the things that I learned and the friendships that I had established in my church family. So, I cannot stress strongly enough how important that support system was for me.

It was especially important when I was 15 and 16 years old. My sister with whom I had been especially close to had met the man with whom she wanted to share her life. That meant that she would be moving out and although I was happy for her, psychologically it was hurting me and scaring me deep inside. I had since the age of six believed that I was the man of the family and was therefore responsible for the care and protection of my sister and mother. I understood later on that this way of thinking was really unreasonable and it had been unintentionally been cemented into my mind from the time I was told by that well-intentioned pastor that I was the man of the family. Sadly, I began to do things that I had been taught not to do. My first mistake was distancing myself from God. I stopped praying and grew less interested in spending time with my church friends or even going to church. I began stealing from stores or the better term would be shoplifting. It wasn't that I needed any of the things I was taking, it was really a cry for help for which I had no idea I needed.

There was the pressure I felt from my sister leaving us, irrational as that was because she wasn't moving overseas, just somewhere else in town. There was the pressure I could sense from my mother that it was time for us to look for a different place to live because we had been with my Grandparents for 10 years since my father's death. Now mind you, there was not any pressure from my Grandparents but it was the passive/aggressive statements that were spoken by other members of the family. After all, they wanted to come visit their Parents and Grandparents in their home without us being there. This was understandable and yet stressful and painful because financially we could not afford to do that during this time. My mother was having to pay a great deal of money for my sister's wedding and although it wasn't a huge wedding, the costs mounted and left over very little for us to plan a move at that time. But God knew what was going on and as always, His plans are better than ours we just have to trust and wait on His movement in our lives sometimes.

Thankfully I was caught and arrested for the shoplifting. This felt terrible but that was a good thing because the weight of the guilt I was feeling was even worse. It was a scary situation being 15 years old, being handcuffed, and taken to jail and put in the holding cell. My mother had to come and get me which I know was embarrassing for her but she was worried about the "why" of it all also. I had to go to court and was ordered to get counseling which turned out to be beneficial because all of those feelings of my fear of not being a very good "man of the family" were addressed and helped me to get myself back on track with my relationship to God. He had never left me, I was that one who had stopped communicating with Him. Even when I was doing what I knew to be wrong there was that still, small voice inside telling me what I was doing was wrong.

My Mother's Mother or Grandma Myra as we called her was never a very close relationship for me. I loved her but she was very different from my other Grandmother with whom we lived. She was older and life had hardened her in many ways. It always seemed to me that we were "in the way" when we were visiting

217

her. She was not mean, she just never seemed to care very much about our lives or what was going on in them. We would visit her with my Mother because we enjoyed the little trips "to the country" and visiting other relatives while we were there. She only lived about 50 miles from where we lived and it was fun to see the area where my mother had grown up and like I just said we had other relatives, cousins, Great Aunts and Uncles that were entertaining and very hospitable that we greatly enjoyed visiting.

When I was 17 years old my Grandmother's health began to deteriorate rather rapidly and she passed away in the fall of that year, the year that my sister had gotten married and moved out. Remember that I said God always knows what is best and He knew that we were needing to move out of our Grandparents home and find a place of our own? Well, it just so happened that my Grandma Myra had left my Mother a small amount of money in her Will and it was enough for us to find a home of our own. It was the first home my Mother had ever owned in her whole life and she was so proud of it. It was a small home of 1200 square feet on a corner lot with a big back yard and just perfect for us. We fenced in the back yard and made lots of improvements to make it our little home. I loved being in charge of the yard and garden area, and of course I had to have a dog, so I felt very blessed and happy.

There have been times in my life that I have physically experienced the holy spirit communicating to me in time of need. I want to share with you one of them. My Mother and I had been living in our new home for about a year when one morning I was awakened by loud crying from my mother in the other room. Of course, I immediately got out of bed and went to see what was wrong. My mother had a condition that most of her life she would grind her teeth at night and other times and over the years she had basically worn her teeth down. As a result, her front two teeth had been capped and glued into place. Sometime during her morning shower, they had come loose and fell out of her mouth and she believed they had washed down the drain. So, she was so distressed because even with her teeth ground down she still has a beautiful smile but now there were two toothpick looking pieces of teeth where her front teeth once were. She was a nurse for 45 years but at this time in her life she had moved in her nursing career from simple patient care to administrative work. Which meant she came into contact on a regular basis with new people and she was the first representation of the hospital and I immediately felt the distress along with her. I went into my bedroom sat on my bed and asked God to tell me what to do. And just as if He was sitting right there beside me I heard Him tell me to go look in the shower door track. Now I understand that it wasn't an audible voice but like the voice you hear when you're talking to yourself inside your head, but I knew it was Him. So I immediately got up went into the bathroom, looked down into the track of the shower door and there miraculously were her two little teeth. I of course immediately went to my mother and gave them to her and told her what I had done. And we both cried and praised God, she went to the dentist to get them glued back in and on to work and I tried to understand and evaluate what had happened.

That had been an amazing thing that had taken place. I mean I understand now that I shouldn't have been surprised because I had gone to my Father in the time of need and asked for His help and He immediately gave it. Perhaps it was the way it happened that amazed me so. Up until this time being a Born-Again Believer in

Jesus Christ I felt the communication of the Holy Spirit in so many different ways. I was moved by preaching or music or hearing the testimonies of others in their walk with the Lord. I knew the Holy Spirit was real but I had never experienced Him communicating to me in that way. There was no "well Dave what do you think you should do? Maybe just go look around the bathroom and see if you can find something." No, the Holy Spirit gave me exact directions as to what to do, and I did it. It was so simple and yet so amazing.

Now you may not consider that to be something extraordinary but I assure you my mother and I certainly did and it planted the seed and desire in me for more. I would love to tell you that it completely transformed my life, I became a preacher evangelist and spent my life explaining to others what I experienced... But I did not. Oh, I shared it with a few people and they were amazed to a certain extent but life went on and I was distracted by the worlds offerings as you would expect a teenage young man to be.

As time progressed and my friends graduated high school, some of them went away to school but I was unsure of what my desire for a career was. I lived in Columbia South Carolina which is the home of the University of South Carolina so like many of my friends I applied and began my college career there. I was like a fish out of water, I didn't feel like I fit in anywhere. I was no longer a fat kid but a fat older teenager trying to fit into "acceptable" expectations of college life. Wearing the right clothes, attracting the right friends etc. This was very difficult for me as I was fat and we had not gotten to the place in our society where "fat shaming" is not an acceptable way of treating someone. I would occasionally see a friend from church but none of us were in the same classes. And I had the problem of trying to squeeze myself into chairs that were made for normal size people and was too embarrassed to ask for help with that. It wasn't that I didn't have the intelligence to do the work required for my classes it was that I simply hated the pressure of standing out in a crowd in which I wanted to be accepted. As a result, I stopped attending classes and failed my first semester attempt at college. I also stopped attending church on a regular basis. The youth group that I had enjoyed so much had changed to a college group with a lot of new faces and so many of my closest friends had moved on with their lives to other colleges. I had learned so much during these youthful years from the wonderful people who taught and discipled me. However, as I have stated earlier in this book, even as born again believers we are subject to the temptations of the world and I found myself sadly distanced from the once close relationship that I had enjoyed with Jesus.

I forgot about the collaboration with God, how He knows what's best for us and wants to lead us in the direction that will be most beneficial to us. I was young and arrogant and wanted to do my own thing regardless of how the Holy Spirit was continually trying to lead me. I thought my plans were best, I rebelled against the wisdom that God had taught me, and along with the rebellion came consequences that I would regret.

During my first failed semester at college I found a job that I really enjoyed. Looking back, I probably should have taken a job first before attempting college but I went along with all of my friends so as not to feel left behind and also youthfully arrogant enough not to be thought of as someone not smart enough to handle it. Peer pressure tends to follow us regardless of our age. The job wasn't anything extra special other than the fact that I got the opportunity to meet so many people from all walks of life. I began working in a Newsstand right near the Capitol building in Columbia. It was before the days of the internet and everyone needed and wanted information and entertainment. The Newsstand offered newspapers from all over the world, hundreds if not thousands of books and magazines of every type you can imagine. So, you can see why people from all walks of life would come through the doors of this business.

It was fun and amusing to meet these people. I developed simple relationships with many people who became "regulars" who would call and ask us to hold a newspaper for them or look for a certain book. I could literally write a book about all of my experiences at the Newsstand but the point that I want to make is that it continued to entice me farther away from my communication and relationship with God. I found myself going to the bar next door after work and having a "few" drinks with some of my co-workers. I began smoking "pot" or "weed" as they refer to it today in order to escape the reality of the sadness I was feeling from distance from God. You may have heard the saying; "If you don't feel close to God, guess who moved?" Well, this was very true at this point in my life.

I had been living with two close friends in a home that was located downtown not too far from the University. It was owned by one of these friend's father and he gave us a great rent to make it easier for us who were going to school. Well, since I had flunked the first semester and stayed out the second semester, it was becoming apparent that without me going to school I would need to find another place to live or go back to school. Of course, I decided to go back to school. As I had given God the perfect right to discipline me as His adopted son, He did so. I got a "whipping" so to speak, which was needed and although not welcomed at the time, I recognized my stupidity and worked on repairing my relationship with my Heavenly Father. And of course, His arms were open wide, and His forgiveness freely given because He knew that my heart had become truly repentant of the stupid things I had done.

I left my job at the Newsstand not because it was a bad place to work, it was the temptations that it offered me that I needed to remove. I went back to USC but this time I had a purpose other than just filling a seat or going because my peers were attending. I became a music major seeking to learn what I could do with the talent God had given me with my voice. Of course, they don't just let you in, I had to apply and audition but I was accepted and began the beginning of a path that I knew God was directing. This was a great new experience for me because even though I was still a fat young man, self-conscious of my size, I felt more at ease and accepted. My professors took notice of my talent and I began to receive encouragement to succeed.

And it just so happened that being a fat music student had its benefits. One day as I was walking down the main hallway of the school I was stopped by the Dean of the School of Music. He asked me if I would be willing to play Santa Claus for the upcoming Christmas pageant that the school put on each year at the Carolina Coliseum. I didn't have to think twice, I accepted immediately and he instructed me to go to the theater department to get measured and suited up for the big day. It really wasn't all that big of a deal, after all, no one would know it was me other than those to whom I shared my excitement. Mainly all I was to do was to ride out in the sleigh and wave to the kids and do some "Ho Ho Ho's" to basically ring in the Christmas at the end of the pageant. After all was said and done and I had shaken the last hand, said "Merry Christmas," told all of the little ones to "go to bed early on Christmas Eve," I was done. Oh, and I forgot to mention that I had perfected imitating the voice of the Santa Claus of which I had heard growing up. You know the one, remember "Rudolph the Red Nosed Reindeer" and the Santa voice… "Rudolph…. That nose, that beautiful red nose". I had unexpectedly become the perfect impersonation of the Jolly old Elf himself. I was proud of my accomplishment and thankful to God for leading on a path that allowed me to experience that amazing time. However, I discovered that there was more in store that I could have never imagined.

I went back to where I had changed my clothes to dress up as Santa only to find that there was no one there to which I was to return the Santa suit. I wasn't going to just leave it there, I was responsible for it, so I took it home and called the school the next day only to find out everyone had gone on Christmas leave at the theater department. They said to just hold onto it until the next semester, after all it wouldn't be needed again until next year. And so, I did.

I had a dear friend who was and is still an amazing pianist and we loved working together. He had accompanied me many times when I would sing in Church, or just coming over to my Mother's house and playing her piano and us all singing and having a blast. He found out that I still had the Santa suit and suggested that I come and sing at the restaurant where he worked. It was one of the finest in town, known for its great Chef and atmosphere and he was sure they would be happy to have me come in and "make merry" for their customers. He secured the ok for a trial run and I showed up ringing my bells, and "Ho Ho Ho-ing" but this time the whole restaurant seemed to stop and take notice when I began to sing some Christmas carols. Not to sound arrogant but I am not just your average singer and when you hear a good singer you know it. I don't have to tell you that my friend Jeff, the pianist was very pleased as his tip jar certainly increased that night, and better for me, I was offered a "gig" to come and sing for the busy nights for the rest of the holiday season. And it wasn't just the singing that I enjoyed, it was going to every table in the place and talking with the customers. In fact, I received a few tips all my own when a few times I was taken aside and asked to deliver a special gift to someone sitting at their table. And one time it was a diamond ring because the gentleman was asking the young lady to be his wife and who better during the Christmas season than to have Santa himself hand her the little gift-wrapped box that would change both of their lives!

Driving home, I remembered the event with tears streaming into my beard thinking of how much I enjoyed giving her that box even though it wasn't actually a gift from me. I was taken back in my mind to when I had received a gift of so much more importance in my own life that Jesus himself had offered and I had accepted. I was really enjoying playing Santa and bringing smiles to everyone's faces, after all, who doesn't enjoy Santa, even the big kids.

And then it hit me. I'm Santa Claus, at least doing a good job of imitating him and who was Santa invented for? That's right, the little kids. So, my plan went into overdrive. I began calling all of the daycare centers in the area and asked if they would like a visit from Santa, of course for a small fee. And boy did they take me up on it. Of course, it didn't hurt that I could tell them that I was the "Singing Santa" that had been written up in the State Newspaper. Apparently one of the customers of the restaurant was a writer and wanted to do a "special interest" piece for the newspaper and I was ready, willing, and able. It was a great little article with my picture, as Santa of course, and the story of how I came to be the "Singing Santa" for the restaurant. The restaurant owner loved the publicity also I might add.

And although I loved doing the "gig" of the "Singing Santa," I fell in love with all the little wide-eyed children at the daycare's who went into what I call "Santa Awe" when I would come in ringing my bells. But the biggest blessing of all was reminding every child that would sit on my knee (Santa had lost his lap years ago), of the real meaning of Christmas. We were celebrating the Greatest Gift that God had given, the birth of His Son Jesus. I can't tell you how many times I was stopped on my way out the door by the director of the daycare thanking me for reminding them of the message of the birth of Jesus being what Christmas was truly all about. That was a great beginning to my 18-year career of playing Santa. I truly miss the old guy sometimes and would probably still be putting on the red suit and ringing my bells had my back not decided that those days would not last forever.

I knew I wanted to continue to study music but still the University of South Carolina's Music School was still so very big and I felt like just a number. So I decided to attempt to go to a school somewhere else in the state. I went and talked to a very nice man at Furman University in Greenville as I had several cousins who had attended that school, however, after an open honest discussion with this gentleman he encouraged me to check out a smaller more personal Junior College in the area, and I am so thankful that he did. It was a school named North Greenville Junior College at the time; it has since grown into a larger

University. But it was perfect for me because the whole student body was about 600. Therefore, the classes were smaller and they had a great little music department. I applied and was accepted in the fall of 1984 and began one of the best semesters of my college career. I met friends that would last my lifetime and learn very much about my voice and how to use it properly. However, like I have explained before, we live in a fallen world and temptations and unexpected tragedies still come which is why it is so important to keep a close personal relationship with Jesus, all the time.

I was keeping an A average in all my classes, I was loving being a part of this small Christian community where everyone knew or knew of each other, especially in our small Music School. Everyone was looking forward to the Christmas break, I had done very well on all of my exams and was preparing for my "jury" which is when you sing in front of the music faculty to show what you have learned over the semester. And then I got a call from home. My Grandmother had had a massive brain stroke and wasn't expected to live very long as a result. Needless to say, I was excused from my further responsibilities at school. They were very understanding knowing that I was very close to my Grandmother and I immediately left for Columbia.

This would be my last Grandmother to pass away. My Grandma Myra had died but her death was expected due to her age and that she had basically given up wanting to live. It still saddened me when she died, I had spent many afternoons with her at the nursing home, just being with her. She didn't talk very much but was glad I was there and I would read to her and just let her know that I cared. But my Grandma Gladys had been such an influence in my life. I had grown close to her over the years. She had taught me so much about how to live out your love of Jesus to others. How many times I can't recall that she would ask me to go with her to some family's home to deliver something. She never made a big deal about it she just gave when she saw someone in need. Many times, people she had met would show up at the house where she would quietly give them money or a bag of food stuffs. Quietly so as not to let Grandad know because he would have had a few things to say about her giving away too much. Don't get me wrong, Grandad was generous to a fault too, but it was mostly with his family.

Grandma had her stroke on the 18th of December as she and Grandad were preparing to go out to dinner at their favorite restaurant, Red Lobster. They were celebrating 62 years of marriage and their relationship had taught me so very much. They had married when she was 15 years old and Grandad was 19 years old and they had determined then and there that this was a lifelong commitment. And they like every other couple had their share of hard times and cross words but they stayed together no matter what. They had a love that was not showy or all romantic and "lovey-dovey" but you could tell that they had learned to love each other in spite of the idiosyncrasies they each new about each other. They still kissed goodnight for as long as I could remember and Grandma gave me advice for when I got married. She would say, "Never go to bed angry, it's better to forgive and get over it." And she would quote a scripture;

"Be angry, and do not sin: do not let the sun go down on your wrath," Ephesians 4:26 (NKJV)

She was the "matriarch" of my Father's family and Christmas was her favorite time of year. Sometimes decorating up to midnight Christmas Eve in anticipation of the whole family coming over the next day for Christmas dinner and gift giving. She loved passing out all the gifts to each and every person in the family, she never forgot anyone and I would know because I spent many a Christmas Eve after watching midnight Mass on the television and "lighting in the Christ Child" as she would describe it. Remember all the windows of that big house? Well, she had to have a candelabra thingy in almost every window upstairs with real burning candles. Talk about a fire hazard! But it was beautiful, and after we would light them all we would go outside and walk down the driveway to see what it looked like from the road. And she had been doing this for quite some time, as even when I was a little thing I recall my mother telling me about how they went out to the road to look at the candles only to notice that one of them had apparently been place too close to the curtains and there were the curtains going up in flames with my Grandad and Father sitting in the same room watching television totally oblivious! Thankfully it was a small enough fire that they got it out but it was a story that would be told every year that I can remember and even she herself would chuckle about it. But it did in no way deter her from putting those candles up every year.

They did that until they were basically forced to move from the big house that I grew up in because they had been attacked by an intruder. A man found an unlocked window in the home and had climbed in. He was apparently on drugs or alcohol and thought that this was my Grandfather's brother's home. My Grandfather's brother had a business that he paid his workers in cash and had a safe in the home where he kept a good sum of cash and this fellow mistakenly thought it was my Grandparents home. To make a long story short, he beat them severely hurting my Grandmother's back and bloodying my Grandfather as he had initially fought the intruder. They were a spry old couple and fought back but to no avail. After several hours of him holding them hostage at gunpoint after finding my Grandfather's gun in his nightstand and searching the house for valuables when he wasn't paying attention, they locked themselves in the upstairs bathroom.

The door to the bathroom was solid wood with a panel in the middle and when the burglar couldn't force it, he went and found an axe and began chopping through the panel. My Grandparents were strong in their faith and they had been praying and they told us how God had instructed them to make a plan. Grandma would wash out her "dainties" in the bathroom sink and subsequently had a bottle of Clorox next to it. She got a glass of Clorox and the burglar saw her doing something and asked her what she was doing and she said, "My husband needs some water, can't I give him a glass of water?" At that point Grandad looked at Grandma and said, "God told me to go on him". Now Grandad had played a lot of football in his younger years and Grandma knew what he meant. He told her that when he tackled this guy for her to run out the house to the neighbors which was a very long distance with her painfully broken back but nonetheless, they were following God's plan.

SO, when the fellow left the bedroom, they came out of the bathroom but the guy met them at the bedroom door. This is when Grandma threw the glass of Clorox in his face and Grandad tackled him. Grandma shut, locked the door, and took off towards the music room to the veranda which is ten feet off of the ground.

Grandad said he could see the fire coming out of the gun as the guy was taken by surprise at the strength of this old man. The gun was fired three times, only by the grace of God not hitting Grandad. And when he heard the "click" the fourth time he tried to fire, he took off running towards the door, stole their car and took off.

Grandma had heard the gunshots as she was running and praying. She got to the lowest point of the roof back by the built-on bedroom and jumped, I am sure it was painful but she made it and got across the street to the neighbor's house where they called the police.

Around 4:00am my mother and I received a call from Grandad saying, "Bring your gun and come because we have been attacked". I am sure he was in shock due to everything they had gone through but it didn't take us long to hurriedly get dressed and of course grab my shotgun (like I was going to have to use it) and speed our way to their home.

When we got there of course the police had already arrived and an ambulance had taken my Grandparents to the hospital where they were checked over and by the grace of God received no serious injury released to come back home. I was amazed at what had taken place and of course curious asking the police a lot of questions. In fact, I helped them find the bullets that had been fired as evidence against this crazy man that had tried to kill my Grandparents. One had gone through the closed bedroom door and lodged in a cushion on a stool sitting by the door. Another had gone into the floor by the stairs and another a few feet away in the wall, showing how Grandad's tackling had forced the guy backwards away from the bedroom.

This event had a devastating effect on my Grandparents, physically as well as psychologically. They didn't feel safe living there by themselves any longer so my sister and brother-in-law moved in with them for a time. And even though one of my cousins had paid to have a security system installed in the home, occasionally it would go off due to a branch against a window from the wind, or someone forgetting it was armed and opening a door, it was still just too much for them to handle so they decided to move. And as God had planned the house right next door to my Aunt, their only daughter came available and they bought it and moved there. And this was such a blessing to my Grandparents as well as my Aunt's family.

And I can say that this was God's plan all along because He and only He has the power to turn something bad that happens into good. So many times in our lives we face trials and difficulties that were so unexpected and horrific and where Satan's plan is to kill and destroy, God turns it into good because He promises to and He cannot lie. I have seen in other's lives as well as my own so many times this scripture made manifest.

"And we know that all things work together for good to those who love God, to those who are the called according to His purpose." Romans 8:28 (NKJV)

My Grandmother had been put on a respirator and the doctors believed that her stroke had been so massive that as soon as it was removed, she would pass away very quickly. So, the decision was made by Grandad and my Aunt and Uncle to remove it. But for some reason I didn't believe that her brain was completely dead. I had spent a few days visiting with her as the family had taken turns staying with her, when we could and I had continually talked with her and encouraged her to "wake up". Of course, this was my wishful thinking on the part of my family, understanding that I was grieving and needed to believe that she would.

So, our big family gathered together in her hospital room. Everyone was crying but for some reason I wasn't. I was convinced that there was still some cognitive connection and she just wasn't ready to leave this world yet. So, I stood in the corner as they had removed her respirator, expecting her to stop breathing at any moment. My Uncle was telling her that the whole family was there and it was ok for her to go ahead and leave, but she didn't. I remember saying, "She's not ready to go yet" and many of my family just looked at me like I was crazy.

Well, she didn't die. Not that day at least, and that was a mystery to the doctors. A mystery to most of our family because a massive brain stem stroke and no brain activity that they could see should have ended her life pretty quickly without the aid of a respirator, and yet she continued to breathe on her own, still unconscious but somehow I knew that she was aware that we were there.

We took turns as a family staying with her, even though the nights even though Christmas was only a few days away. I had asked to stay with her on Christmas Eve as we had spent so many of them together and I realized that this would probably be the last one I would spend with her. They brought a small cot into the room for us to use and although I tried to stay awake all night, I would nod off every now and then. I would talk with her and massage her feet and then she would stop breathing, and my heart felt like it had stopped too. I think God knew that me actually being there when she died would have been pretty hard on me so my cousin came in early Christmas morning to take my place and I sleepily made my way back to my Grandad's home and fell asleep.

At about 1:00pm I was awakened with the news that my Grandmother had breathed her last breath and had gone to be with her Lord and Savior Jesus Christ. And we all realized that the whole family was together, just as it was every Christmas when we would eat at around 1:00pm for Christmas dinner. She had chosen just the right time to leave this earth and God had granted that gift to her family as we all needed to be together to mourn and celebrate this woman that had been so special to each one of us in her own unique way.

I share these things with you in the hope that you find that everyone experiences sadness and death, trials and tribulations in their lives but it's how you handle them and who you depend upon when these events occur in life that is most important. As a born-again believer in Jesus my sadness is combined with joy and peace because of my faith and trust in what I know to be true and have experienced over and over again.

I went back to North Greenville Junior College and stayed there for the next year and a half. The death of my Grandmother had an unexpected effect on me and I lost interest in my studies, played too much, did things of which I am ashamed, suffice it to say that the Holy Spirit doesn't get "high" or "drunk" and there were too many times that He would ask me "Why are you doing this?" When God is speaking to me, He doesn't beat around the bush but talks directly to your spirit and was always with me, wanting me to come back to Him and continue the collaboration we had begun when I was nine years old. After too many mistakes to mention, too many times I listened to my own desires regardless of God's urging to do the opposite, I determined to leave college and go back home.

My loving Mother of course welcomed me back with open arms, understanding that I was still without direction and needed time to determine what I wanted to do with my life, and without her unconditional love and prayers I doubt you would be reading this now. In short, it took a while and a great deal more of paths not designed by God, but He never left me or gave up on me because He always knew my heart. Remember how I stated that we can't disappoint God because He always knows what we are going to do? And many times, He will allow us to venture down dangerous roads and let us experience pain and hard times that He can turn into growing experiences that may be needed for future events. And He did just that. And it led me to a place where I wanted to continue my music career. So, I trusted His direction and He led me to a College in Nashville Tennessee now known as Belmont University.

I was somewhat the "odd man out" going to Belmont College at the age of 27. Most of the other students were just coming out of High School or from Junior Colleges, however, I made many friends and in fact had a few that had come from North Greenville College. It was a great time because I felt I was once again collaborating or "in Gods will." I was majoring in Commercial Vocal Performance and I had met and become friends with a professor there that had lived in Columbia also growing up. In fact, his father had been the Minister of Music at the church I grew up in and had left just before we became members there. We formed a friendship beyond just his teaching me and I was the beneficiary of many fun times spent with him and his beautiful talented wife, and their three four legged children. They were dog lovers as was I and they had three beautiful Akita's that I got to "dog sit" on many occasions.

It was during this time at Belmont that I met who, unbeknownst to me, would become the love of my life, my best friend and the greatest gift on this earth God could have given me, my wife Shelley. It was very strange how I had no initial attraction to her, actually I thought her to be just a little weird. Now that I think back on it, if I would have recognized that our "weirdness" was so alike we were the perfect match. She became a friend and I recall specifically one evening as we were sitting in a Burger King on Broadway that she and one of her friends were asking me questions about one of my friends. She was interested in him and wanted to know if I thought that he might be interested in her. I attribute this next part directly to the Holy Spirit because I literally had never thought of her in a romantic way. The thought, "why would you be interested in him when I am sitting right in front of you" ran through my mind. Of course, little did I know that she would turn out to recognize how wonderful I was and perfect for her, but that would be years later. I say this humorously although I have always remembered to pay attention when a strange thought that I attribute to myself crosses my mind, just to make sure it's not a suggestion the Holy Spirit is planting for future use. And He most assuredly has as I have been the beneficiary of many "directions" by Him throughout this adventure called life, and the collaboration I have enjoyed with His Lordship of my life.

I learned a lot about my talent at Belmont which is really the reason you should seek higher education. Practical application of a skill or talent makes all the investment worthwhile as I discovered. My friend/professor was also in the music business as well as being a professor and recommended me for a job with a band that was looking for a singer. Sadly, I had to drop out of Belmont during one of my best semesters there. It seemed as if I was not to ever receive a diploma but what I was about to receive made up for it. In short, when I had gone to North Greenville College I had made student loans and of course I also made them at Belmont, however, the loans were not exactly the same so while one loan knew I was still I school, the other loan of which I thought I was in deferment standing, I was not and due to my error they defaulted my financial aid. I couldn't attend without financial aid and subsequently even though I had gone so far as to involve my US Senators office in the problem, the school would not let me take my exams until the debt was paid. And as a result, I received zero's in all my classes but one, hilariously it was a class on Golf which I had already made an A in, and after a time all of those zero's turned into "F's" which made me look like I had flunked out of school. But God had a way of turning bad into good as He always promised.

I auditioned for the band and was hired. It was a Big Band that travelled from Nashville all over the country but mostly the Southeast as the owner was from Rocky Mount North Carolina and was a retired Brigadier General from the Army. He loved music and was a great presence on stage and had made a name for himself in the Music business for what his band offered. We did mostly society/charity, wedding receptions, political functions, conventions, and even a few Presidential Inaugural Balls, etc., and were well known for being great at what we did. It consisted of a 15-piece band and three singers, well four if you count the owner who was Bo Thorpe. So, the name of the band was "Bo Thorpe and his Orchestra". I am sure you haven't heard of it but on the off chance there it is. I am sure he wouldn't mind me mentioning his name, he was a "ham" and a lover of attention, a purple heart recipient, and an all-around good fellow. He passed away several years ago but during my time with the band I made it a point to ask him about his relationship to God and if he was born again. Happily, he answered in the affirmative so I am expecting to see him again one day!

Working with that band was one of the best experiences of my life. I got to go places that I probably never would have otherwise travelled to, much less stayed at; But such was the nature of the business. We would perform at huge conventions with a famous act on one end of the giant room and us on the other. The "famous" person would perform for about an hour and we would provide dance/party music for the rest of the evening and sometimes our band would be the band for the famous entertainer. I got to work with some wonderfully talented people also. The lady singer who had been with the band about five years when I joined had experienced an amazing career herself. She had sung with Harry James, Frank Sinatra Jr., Tommy and Jimmy Dorsey, just to name a few. She was beautiful, and just as talented as she looked with a loving heart and kindness for everyone she met. She and her husband had come to Nashville from Las Vegas where they had worked for years. Her husband was an amazing musician himself and played saxophone, as well as being a brainiac and owning his own computer business. We had another male singer with whom I would grow very close. We spent a lot of time together and shared life's challenges, laughed a lot, cried some too, but enjoyed singing and performing together. He would later agree to become my Best Man at our wedding. It was great fun, but challenging too. Open bars at many of the events became temptations that I fell right into and let's just say that my Christian witness was mostly unnoticeable I am sad to say.

I travelled with this band for almost eight years also doing other jobs because as a free-lance musician just working with the band didn't pay all the bills let's just say. But it was during this time that even though I had left Belmont, I had kept in touch with Shelley and we had become close friends. We would go to movies and out to eat, but never really considered them "dates." No, I was too stupid to recognize how amazing a woman she was and how perfectly we fit together. We could and would talk about everything for hours and hours. We would laugh and just enjoy each other's companionship. As I look back on it now, if I had not been so afraid of commitment and the responsibility I knew that marriage required, I would not have waited so long to ask her to marry me. But remember, never take God out of the equation and He had a plan that would work out in spite of my stupidity. And praise His Holy name, He always does! That's why I call it a collaboration. God isn't a task master forcing us into things, He lovingly, willingly, is always ready to lead us but it is according to our willingness to follow that lead. There can't be two Lords of your life as I have regrettably experienced too many times to mention. But the story continues…

Shelley had graduated and received her degree in Music from Belmont. She was and still is an amazing talented singer and since she didn't see me moving towards asking her to marry me, she decided to move on with her life. She enjoyed singing Jazz and Nashville isn't really known for its Jazz music so she decided to give New York City a try. She had a friend at the Olive Garden where she was working whose mother lived just outside of the city and was willing to rent her a room. Now my Shelley is talented, determined, gutsy, and smarter than even she gives herself credit, and she made her plans and asked me if I would help her to move and she did!

She had yard sales, saved up her money, rented a U-Haul truck, got me to drive the truck with her following behind in "Ruby" her little red Ford Taurus. Her parents were not really all that pleased with this move as it was a great deal farther away from them living in Saint Augustine Florida, but they knew what their little girl was made of and supported her in any way they could. They bought my return ticket after we got her set up in Dobbs Ferry which is the little town in which she would be living.

We got to Dobbs Ferry settled her in and took off for a day and night of sightseeing in New York. I had secured tickets to see the David Letterman show through a friend of Bo Thorpe's who I'll just say was famous enough to do so, and so we had a great two days there. But boy was it hard for me to say goodbye. It's like my heart knew that we were supposed to be together but my stupid mind was fighting it. I didn't have anything to offer her, after all I was just a poor free-lance musician, not to mention that I was not an "Adonis"? No in fact I was just a 400- pound wanna be successful musician with dreams and aspirations but I could hardly support myself, much less a wife and I believed she deserved much better than what I had to offer. Once again, go ahead and laugh, here I am KNOWING not to take God out of the equation and yet I chose to let her move away not knowing if I would ever have the chance to have her back again. I loved her and she loved me but I was lost in the battle of heart and mind.

I went back to South Carolina and stayed with my Mother for a while, still traveling to wherever the Bo "gigs" were. I called Shelley one day and told her that I needed some time to get my head together and basically that she shouldn't wait on this to happen. I didn't really mean to sound like I was breaking our relationship, but then again it is what I was doing. This really hurt her and subsequently her father put out a contract on me, no I am just kidding, but let's just say that I was "persona non grata" as far as they were concerned and understandably so. I just knew that I had to make sure that if we were supposed to be together that I had to figure out what I needed to do to make it happen and I was struggling with that. But God…

I then decided to move up to Wilmington North Carolina where my Sister's little family lived. They invited me, or I invited myself to live with them for a while and worked at a furniture store with them and enjoyed playing Uncle for my wonderful little niece and nephew. And I think this is where my desire to be a husband and a father took root. I got to see, the good, the bad, and the ugly, that marriage entails. And yet through that lens I got to see my sister and brother-in-law and their commitment and through struggles that they loved each other in spite of it all; and I could see myself doing that also. Well, it just so happened that we had a "Bo gig" going to New York City coming up in the later Summer of that year. I began to make my plan.

My sister had a beautiful ring that my mother had given her on her 18th birthday. It was a ring that my mother had inherited from her mother and it had a really cool history. My Grandfather had worked on a streetcar in Savannah Georgia when my mother was a little girl and had found the setting of a ring on the street car. It was a beautiful filigree ring that was missing a stone. So my Grandfather had a semi-precious stone called a "spinel" put in the ring, then put it in his coat pocket and told my Grandmother he had a hole in the pocket and asked her to repair it, and that is how he surprised her with it. Well, my sister liked the stone but not the ring so much so she had the stone removed and made into a pendant. But I wanted this ring to use as an engagement ring for Shelley, but there was no way I could afford a diamond, much less at least a one or two carat diamond that this ring needed so I asked my sister if I could have the original stone back to put back into the ring and if I could have it to give to Shelley as an engagement ring. She agreed, and was excited for me, so I took the stone and had it put back in the ring.

During all of this time God was working in Shelley's life in New York. She went through a few different jobs, some famine times, and even close to a recording deal with a Jazz label, but that was not to be because God had a plan for her to influence and be influenced by a wonderful Jewish family for which she became the "Nanny". She was answering ads to find work when she came across one for this family needing a Nanny. They had two small girls and the Mother was pregnant with a third and it looked like a good fit. And of course, God had planned it all along. Shelley fell in love with the family and they with her. They eventually invited her to come and live with them in their basement of this huge home and she was happy to do so. The interesting thing for Shelley was that she got to experience the Jewish lifestyle for over a year meaning that she got to celebrate all of the feasts and festivals. She often talks about how she learned more about Jesus from this Jewish family than from years of just going to church. You see the Jewish feasts and festivals point to and emphasize the Messiah who is Yeshua, the Hebrew name for Jesus.

Back to what I was trying to figure out, the problem if Shelley would even see me in New York. I had determined that if she would see me, perhaps come to our "gig", maybe go out after and just spend some time together… and it all went well, then I knew that I would ask her to marry me, but not then and not there. I laugh when I am tempted to say, "it just so happens", or "coincidentally" because I know God is always working behind the scenes and many times right in front of your eyes, preparing you for things. So, as God planned it Shelley was agreeable to come to our "gig" in New York. She showed up at my hotel room at just the right time looking gorgeous. We had been talking over the phone for some time again so it wasn't as awkward as you might think. We went to our "gig" at the Waldorf Astoria Hotel and it was a beautiful evening. All of the band members knew what I was planning and were happy to meet Shelley without ever saying anything about my plans to eventually ask her to marry me.

After the "gig" I took Shelley to a nice restaurant for a midnight meal. We talked and laughed and I had figured out a way to secretly find out her ring size. I had on this pinky ring that she saw and thought it odd because she knew that I was not a big fan of jewelry, so I got her to try it on and it was a perfect fit. Great little idea if I do say so. Now I secretly had her ring size to get the ring sized to. We spent the next few hours wandering around the "city that never sleeps," we even went to a piano bar where I tipped the pianist to play "It had to be You" and I sang that to her, there at whatever time in the early morning hours, in a piano bar in New York City, it was indeed romantic. We went back to my hotel room that I was sharing with another band member and stayed up most of the rest of the night just talking and giving me the opportunity to sincerely apologize for making her think that I had abandoned her and could we continue our relationship, albeit long distance from this point forward.

Thankfully she was agreeable, and in her mind, we were just picking up where we left off. In my mind, I couldn't wait to marry her!

God arranged that I had some close friends who had a son about my nephews age and they were planning a trip to Orlando to go to Disney etc. and wanted to know if my nephew and I would like to come stay in their "time share" with them. My nephew and I would drive down to Orlando and pick them up at the airport. And God planned it that during that exact same week, Shelley was going to be in Saint Augustine for her ten-year High School reunion. So, I made the plan that we would do our week in Orlando and my nephew would ride back with my friends because they wanted to rent a car to do sight-seeing on the way back, it was all working out perfectly. Then I was free to stop by Saint Augustine to see Shelley and ask her to marry me.

It was all working out great. I had gotten the ring sized and the stone re-mounted. I had planned on asking her to marry me at one of the gun turrets on the famous Bridge of Lions there in Saint Augustine. I had memorized my proposal speech and had even written it down in a letter for her just in case during the craziness of the moment she wouldn't remember it. I came into town and got my hotel room. I had scheduled an early evening dinner with Shelley because I wanted to be on the Bridge at Sunset, I know right, I am a true romantic but you aint' seen nothing yet! I even remembered to stop and get some flowers for Shelley but also for her mother because she really didn't like me at this point but I knew that if everything worked out to plan, she would eventually have to, right? I would definitely have to trust God with that.

I got to Shelley's house, went in and gave the flowers to her and her mother, who gave me the really cold shoulder and we left for dinner. I was as nervous as I could be. I had the ring in my pocket but was terrified that one wrong move and there goes the ring bouncing off of the bridge into the bay, gone forever, so it was my mission to get that ring on her finger as soon as possible. But it looked like storm clouds were brewing in the distance so we quickly found a parking space and I hurriedly forced Shelley up the bridge to the spot I had picked out. She had no idea what was going on, I had just told her that I wanted to see the sunset from the bridge and we needed to hurry before any rain may come. So, we get to the spot and I begin my speech. "Shelley, I have a gift that I would like to give to you. My Grandfather gave it to my Grandmother, my Grandmother gave it to my Mother, my Mother gave it to my Sister, and my Sister gave it to me to give to you, and I would like to keep it in the family… will you be my family, will you marry me?" Dead air…nothing…she stared at me as if we were frozen in time. I was amazed myself and confused. I was confident that she would say yes and here we were in an awkward silence that seemed to go on forever. I said again "will you marry me? Will you be my wife?" And then I think it hit her, I had totally surprised her with this proposal, something I had always wanted to do and she was really surprised. In her mind we were just beginning our relationship again and this was just a date. Finally, she said the words I had been longing to hear "Yes" as she wrapped her arms around me and I said wait let's get this ring on your finger before I drop it into the ocean.

I also had written a song for her, but I can't remember when I sang it to her, I know it wasn't on the bridge, nonetheless I will share the words here so you can be impressed with how romantic I was back then…I still have my moments although few and far in between. The title is "As I Love You"

If you could look into my heart and know that every part
    Is filled with a love that is true.
Or read the thoughts within my mind, for each moment in
time, would be filled with a memory of you.

Or crawl under my skin, feel the tingle begin
    As I gaze deeply into your eyes… would you love me?
Could you love me?

If I would climb the highest mountain, walk across the driest
desert, and then swim the deepest sea.

Bottle moon beams and sunlight, capture rainbows and starlit
nights, to show how much you mean to me.

If I could stop the seasons changing, make the sunshine when
it's raining, turn the moon to a royal blue…could you love me?
Would you love me…
    As I love you?

But I have only love to offer, not a kingdom or a crown.
    For I'm neither prince nor pauper, just an ordinary clown.
    In a world of fools, I'll break the rules to prove my love for
you.
    It's for you I wrote this heartfelt tune, and for you I would
lasso the moon.

If at the sunset I would squeeze you tight, gently kiss your lips
each night, and then hold you till the dawn.

If I would promise I will always care, never leave always be here,

From this moment on.

In a world constantly changing, let me be your rock to cling to. Let me be your knight in shining armor, the little boy you sing to.

And you can love me, will you love me...

As I love you?

I wish you could hear it with the music but the words say so much of what my heart longed to share with her. I knew that she understood that I really deeply loved her and although it had taken what seemed like forever for me to recognize it, at least I finally had!

I was so thankful that she had accepted, and yet she also knew that we had a few hurdles that were before us. First, we decided to go and tell her Grandmother who lived a short distance away on the island. I can't remember whether we went out to eat first or after but we did go out to a restaurant and made some plans such as when to have the wedding, how we were going to get her from New York to Nashville etc. but first things first, I had to get the blessing of her mother and dad. I think the reason Shelley wanted to go to her Grandmother's first was because she knew her Grandmother couldn't keep a secret, and especially one this big, so she would no doubt be burning up the phone line to tell Shelley's parents the news to give them some time to digest it before we actually got there in person.

When we got to her house, her mother was already in bed, so we made our way to her father's little television room where he was there waiting with shotgun in hand and red eyes blaring. No, of course I am teasing, however our talk was not an easy one. He made it perfectly clear that he was angry with me for hurting Shelley, and he drug me over the coals, so to speak. Shelley was in the laundry room right next to his room, out of sight, praying the whole time. I understood his concern and displeasure but I also knew that even though I desired his blessing that Shelley was 28 years old and I was 33 and we certainly didn't need anyone's permission. But I wanted him to know how much I loved his daughter and convince him that I would always be there for her and that he would eventually see that. And being the wise man that he was, he told me that in no uncertain terms would there ever be any choice ultimatums given. He knew that Shelley would be my wife and there would never be any reason for her to have to choose between me and them. I understood that to mean, "Welcome to the family" and in effect it did. It took some time but eventually they came to love me as their son. They announced our engagement at church the next morning and took us to a really nice restaurant for lunch.

I headed back to Columbia and then on to Nashville a few months later to find us a place to live. I hadn't taken into consideration all of the planning and stuff that goes into a wedding but we got through it. Even over long distance, her living in New York and me living in Nashville. Being a freelance musician and Shelley being a nanny for a family in New York at the time I don't need to tell you that our financial situation was precarious at best. In other words, our credit was poor if nonexistent and being approved to rent somewhere was challenging. One day I was at a session and some of the other musicians and I we're discussing my upcoming marriage to Shelley and I shared with them my frustration in trying to find a place for us to begin our life together. One of my friends who is a great piano player told me of a place he knew that was for rent and suggested I go take a look at it and apply to live there. I got in touch with the property manager went and took a look at it.

Well, as soon as I drove up, I knew that Shelley would fall in love with it when she saw it and I wasn't going to make that decision on my own and thankfully she was getting ready to come into town. So, we made another appointment to go look at it and like I had guessed she fell in love with it and we filled out an application. But we both were discouraged and not too confident that we would be approved. We prayed and asked God to help us to get the place if it was his will, and we started making plans and imagining how it would be to live there and before you know it, she had to go back to New York. When Shelley got back to New York she called me immediately and told me about her flight and how while she was reading in a devotional magazine and it was telling about the time that the two blind men came to Jesus crying out "Son of David have mercy on us" and Jesus said to them "Do you believe that I am able to do this?" Those words spoke to both of us and we prayed together over the phone and said yes Lord we believe. For the next few days I would drive by the house and it was as if I could hear Jesus saying to me through the Holy Spirit, "Do you believe I am able to do this?" I was overwhelmed with the feeling of security and absolute confidence that He could and would. By the end of the week I heard from the property manager that we were approved and what a wonderful feeling it was to call Shelley and tell her. We would spend the first two years of our married life together in that home.

What I learned from that experience was a new desire to discover how these things happened. Jesus did so many miracles

249

and a consistent theme in all of them is the demand from them Jesus required. What I mean is every miracle required faith from the person receiving the miracle or from someone else. The reason I say someone else's because Jesus raised Lazarus from the dead as a result of faith from Mary. It's like I've been saying since the beginning our relationship to God is in fact a collaboration, He works with us and for us but requires our input making us a part of the miracle. Don't get me wrong here it's Jesus that does the miracle but He wants us to know how important our faith, our belief is in the process.

Now we were living in Nashville and Shelley had become a babysitter for some dear friends of ours with whom I had lived up until we got married. They had a beautiful little two-year-old daughter and one day they asked Shelley to come get her and keep her for the day. It wasn't too long after Shelley left the house to go get her that she called me frantic. She had put the little girl in the car seat, hooked her in, closed the door and gone around to get into the truck when she discovered that the door was locked and the keys were in the ignition along with her purse that had my keys to the truck. I am immediately got in to our other car and headed over. Thankfully it was earlier in the morning so the heat of the day hadn't begun and she had been carefully and lovingly talking to the little girl to assure her everything was all right. Our truck was a Ford Ranger. I could see that the little girl trusted us both but was starting to get a little panicky and quite frankly so was I. I began to think the only thing we could do was to bust the window out and that is something I did not want to do because I knew it would scare her and cost of butt load of money to repair. So, I stopped close my eyes and prayed, "Dear God please tell me what to do." That same voice that had spoken to me about where my mother's teeth were told me clearly "Tell the little girl to take her shoe off and her sock and reach down and pull the door handle with her foot." This vehicle was the kind that when you pull the door handle it would unlock, and it did. Shelley had looked at me like I was a little bit crazy at first but then I told her what I had done and she knew that God had once again met our need once again.

Our life together has been full of stories like this. I could go on and on and I will hit some of the high points. We started a house cleaning business there in Nashville and discovered that we loved being together and not working separately. During the Christmas season I would be Santa and she would come and work with me, not as Mrs. Claus but as a helper. After a few years of spinning our wheels, Shelley and I moved to Columbia to help my mother sell her house and move her into a small duplex that was perfect for her. We lived in Columbia until God moved us back up to Brentwood Tennessee to be Houseparent's at the Tennessee Baptist Children's Home there and then on to a satellite home in Johnson City. We were so blessed and tested by the ministry. It was a wonderful seven years that we worked there especially because it was during this time that God led us to go get our daughters who had been born in The People's Republic of China. I could write a whole book about how God used us to touch those girls lives at the Children's Home, how He taught us so much about Himself and loving through every difficulty, even those that you could never imagine. He grew our faith like never before as He made it possible for us to travel to China twice to become the parents of our beautiful talented daughters. And at Christmas both times as if He was showing us that children truly are a gift.

We came back from China with our youngest daughter and our time at the Children's Home ended. But God always has a plan and knew what was on the horizon. We moved to a little town called Thompson's Station just outside of Nashville and rented a house there. My mother became ill and was diagnosed with colon cancer and I was up and down the road to Columbia every time I could get away. She went to be with Jesus in June and 54 days later Shelley's mother passed away after discovering a previous battle with breast cancer had spread. My mother was 77 when she passed but Shelley's mother was only 63, much too young. But God had a plan and instead of us moving Shelley's dad up to Tennessee, which he probably wouldn't have done anyway, we moved down to Saint Augustine to live with him. We got to share our amazing little girls with him for about eight years until he also went to be with the Lord.

Then a few years later after growing tired of trying to keep up the over an acre lot and the pool, and the house, we decided as a family to do something Shelley had wanted to do for a long time. And since the home and land were her inheritance, we did just what she wanted. We sold the home, bought a truck and a fifth wheel and traveled this great Country of ours for 2 years. We went to 34 states, got to see relatives that we hadn't seen in years and Shelley and the girls had never met. We met so many wonderful people and got to share our love of Jesus with them and many shared with us also. We got to see my Uncle right before he passed away and he had been very special in my life so that was another little gift from my Heavenly Father.

We got to go and experience a lot that many will never experience over their lifetime and it was a great educational trip for our girls. Although it wasn't all peaches and cream. There were times of trials and hard times but the Lord as always led us in the way we needed to go. And here I sit, writing this living on Anastasia Island in Saint Augustine Florida during a pandemic. Not thankful for the pandemic but so glad the Lord led us to travel before this thing hit as it would have been a very different world, and perhaps even impossible for us to do. God is always working wanting us to collaborate with Him, to daily die to ourselves and choose to make Him Lord so that He can direct our paths.

Well, that's about it. Thanks for reading and sharing your time with me if you have read this far. Surely you can see how over the past half century I have experienced and amazing journey with THE God of the Universe. There is no way I could have made all this up even with the wild imagination that I have. But as always, it's really all about you and your choices. I made mine back when I was nine years old and I am forever thankful that I did. As a child, with childlike faith, believing God's word.

If you haven't talked to God and asked Him to forgive you for your sins, I encourage you to do so. Jesus loves you more than you can imagine regardless of your situation and He proved it by dying in your place on the cross. More importantly He proved that He was God in the flesh by rising again from the dead. He is real, it's not a fairy tale, or fiction. It's really very simple, it always has been. God loves you and wants you to choose to love Him back. It's your choice.

The End…

or a new beginning!!

About the Author

This is William David Swindler's first book. He has no sophisticated educational degrees, only a desire to share the love of Christ with others. He enjoys reading, debating politics, as well as other issues. But his main passion is discovering more about God and all of His amazing aspects and then driving others crazy with the information. He firmly believes that the scriptures have so much to offer anyone who will dig into them with a desire to discover more about the loving God who truly loves beyond our comprehension.

David, along with his wife Shelley, two daughters Alyson and Liliana, and their two Jack Russell terrorists make their home on Anastasia Island in Saint Augustine Florida. They spent two years travelling this beautiful country full timing in a fifth wheel. It was an amazing adventure and he and his family encourage everyone to discover the magnificence of this wonderful country with which God has so truly blessed us.

If you desire more information about possible future works, or if you would be interested in having him come and share with your church, or any group, please contact him through email wdavidswindler@icloud.com

www.ingramcontent.com/pod-product-compliance
Lightning Source LLC
LaVergne TN
LVHW051459080426
835509LV00017B/1830